Music Is Medicine

Accessing Sacred Wisdom
From the Master Within

by
Martin Klabunde

Music Is Medicine

Accessing Sacred Wisdom
From the Master Within

ISBN-13: 978-0615484914
ISBN-10: 0615484913

Book Website: www.collectiveawakening.us
Email: now@collectiveawakening.us
or collectiveawakening@gmail.com

Facebook: www.facebook.com/martin.klabunde
Twitter: www.twitter.com/martinklabunde

Give feedback on the book at:
now@collectiveawakening.us

Printed in U.S.A

For those seeking inner peace.

May you walk
with gratitude,
forgiveness
and
unconditional love.

Music is Medicine:

Accessing Sacred Wisdom from the Master Within

▣   ▣   ▣

Contents

Contents
(continued)

Contents
(continued)

Contents
(continued)

Our brother is the drum who plays a heart song
  that heals our spirits and opens our voices
  to sing the song within us.
Our brother is the drum who plays an earth song
  that awakens our true nature and ties us to this
  planet, with all its living creatures.
Our brother is the drum who plays a shamanic song
  that speaks to the spirits of the mountains and the
  temples and stirs the drummer in all of us.
Our brother is the drum who plays a memory song
  that moves our bodies in an ancient dance,
  expanding our awareness of tribe, time and place.
Our brother is the drum who plays a universal song
  that reaches to the stars, shining the music of our
  souls back to us, uniting us and making us whole.
Our Brother is the Drum.

- Hunter Black (1952 - 2008)

My dear Hunter, thank you so much for teaching me about
  dedication, devotion and how to be a humble servant.

I would like to extend my appreciation and gratitude to those who have given their energy and support without which this book may not have ever been written.

My mother and father for supporting my passion for music and my dedication in pursuing it.

My wife and best friend, Wing Man Rita Law, for her undying dedication to her own awakening, our partnership and to being a messenger for so many.

Leslee Morrison and Vanessa Morgan for their event and programming support and in lending an eye to the manuscript in the development stages.

Finally, I would like to thank the tribe,
Wymak (the hand),
Felix (the cat),
and Pierre (no doy una)
for all your guidance and support.

INTRODUCTION

I know someone who inspired me . . .

to let go of everything I thought I knew,

to reinvent myself every day,
and to wake up from the ordinary
and jump into to the extraordinary.

I know someone who is completely content
no matter what is happening.

I know someone who knows
that this is the secret to Life.

This someone is inside you.

The Master Within has been waiting
for your acknowledgement
and your surrender.

What a beautiful existence we have as human beings. This wonderful reality of existing in both the physical and spiritual realms simultaneously offers us so many opportunities to deepen our connection to the divine inside each of us. Life is a mirror, a barometer of sorts that presents us with direct experiences that tell us exactly where our spiritual evolution lies. Being human presents us with very clear results that are beneficial when we seek to evolve to a deeper and more meaningful existence. Our existence in this body and on Mother Earth is a result of our spirits' desire to evolve to higher states of being and a desire to exist at a higher vibration. Our human experience is the foundation for future nonphysical endeavors. What we remember here, we will carry with us after our physical body returns to the earth.

Our spirit carries all the knowledge and wisdom we need to elevate to higher levels of consciousness while in this body. This life provides us opportunities to remember this wisdom and integrate it into our physical, mental, emotional, and spiritual bodies, and we have powerful tools of transformation to help us with this adventure of inner exploration. As we walk the path of our inner being, we begin to develop a deeper awareness, detachment, clear intuition and wisdom. We begin to clearly hear the voice of a Master in each of us. This inner guide offers us Sacred Wisdom, and if we choose to listen, our perception transforms, allowing the problems and challenges we experience to fade away.

So, how can we begin to experience the freedom of Sacred Wisdom and the Master Within? How can we create an expanded awareness, a deeper perception, or act with wisdom? How can we remember our history as cosmic walkers, where we are going and how we are going to get there? How can we begin our own transformative path when life seems to be moving so fast or when we just don't know where to begin?

We need something that reminds us of our mission on earth, something that speaks directly to our soul and our spirit and something that helps us stay on track. There is something that resides in both the physical and the spiritual domains that does just that; it is a language that every human understands and that can connect us to a power greater than ourselves. It is music. Music lives in the invisible until we connect with it and bring it into the physical. When we listen to or play music, we connect to our inner being and transport our awareness to unseen dimensions. This experience will alter our perception just enough so that we provide ourselves the opportunity to unite with our inner being. Music is the bridge between the physical and the spiritual, the seen and the unseen, the mortal and the immortal.

Music provides a path of becoming and a powerful tool for connecting with our cosmic memory of the spirit worlds. Music is the language of the spirit; it transcends all spoken languages and connects all humans on an intuitive and spiritual level. Music speaks to our physical, mental, emotional and spiritual bodies and provides us a direct connection to spirit. When we play music in a sacred context, we can discover the Master Within and offer ourselves the opportunity to conspire with the Great Spirit to be a servant to humanity, the Earth and other spirits. If we can remember how to use music for our spiritual evolution, we will have connected with one of the most powerful forms of cosmic communication known to humans.

Music is the medicine, we are the doctors and the world is the patient. Music is a language that the spirit understands clearly, and it resides in a place deep within us that is protected from the constructs of the mind. Music speaks through metaphors, anecdotes and stories. When we listen to or play music, we are free to leave the mundane world and allow our spirits to fly and to access the wisdom needed to experience balance, peace, contentment and serenity. When we play music, we have the opportunity to write our story. We are free to consider, dream and live the possibilities. Maybe, just maybe, we will see that the dream is here and now and that the possibilities are endless.

This book speaks to the human experience as beings living in two worlds, the physical and the spiritual. It addresses our desire to be happy and filled with love and to awaken to the highest level of awareness available to us. This book offers the reader new possibilities in pursuing emotional, mental, and spiritual transformation through the intentional use of music. This book demonstrates how music is our ticket to the greatest show on earth and in the universe, a spectacular performance where we are the performers and where we conspire with the gods to re-create the magic we are born of.

In writing this book, I realize that some of the concepts I present here may seem out of reach or just unbelievable and you may wonder how to apply them to your own life. It is very much like the classic line in so many fantasy stories: "You just have to believe." I have tried to connect them to my own real-life experiences to give them context and demonstrate to the reader that we are capable of existing in two worlds.

We are magical beings and so much more than what we have been told we are. Our parents, grandparents, great-grandparents and so on had a certain level of awareness that was appropriately functional for the time they were living. Naturally, they taught us what they were taught. The times have changed dramatically and the awareness available to us cannot be found by merely abiding by the knowledge our recent ancestors have given us. We have to jump into this new awareness. We have to completely let go of what we think we know and offer ourselves to the revolution that is upon us. This is a revolution of the spirit and now is the time!

CHAPTER ONE

Spirituality: Introducing A New Paradigm

回   回   回

What Is Awakening?

Awakening is the lifting of the veil
that hangs in front of our spiritual eyes.

Awakening is the emergence of new perceptions that
offer new definitions
of freedom, love and life.

Awakening is seeing the possibility
of happiness and deep contentment.

Awakening is turning every moment
into an active meditation.

Awakening is self-realization.

Awakening knows that the universe
supports your life journey.
Awakening is cultivating a deeper connection
with the divine in each of us.

Awakening is being present in every moment.

Awakening is in your smile.

Awakening is having compassion for all people.

Awakening is being tolerant of others.
Awakening is having nothing to protect.

Awakening is remembering how to engage
unlimited and unconditional love.

Awakening is surrendering
to All That Is at this moment.

Awakening knows you are more than your body.

Awakening is strengthening the connection
among your Mind, Body, and Spirit.

Awakening is developing Emotional Freedom.

Awakening is following your path
no matter what.

We are all awakening . . . collectively.

◙   ◙   ◙

Awakening to Your Spirit

Spirituality is our connection to the Divine, a force
within, without, and connected to our physical form.
It is one that we are all a part of, and our collective
humanness offers us the possibility to connect to this
Divinity; it resides inside each of us. We are creations
of Spirit and Earth, the seen and the unseen, the visible

and the invisible, the mortal and the immortal. Spirituality is an active pursuit of the spirit and the connection to the Divinity inside each of us. Spirituality is a sincere desire to serve the Divine with passion, devotion and dedication.

Spirituality is an active participation
in the magic of life.

Divinity manifests as sacred wisdom, an inner knowing of who you are and what your mission on earth is in this lifetime. You were born with this sacred wisdom; it is a part of who you are and a part of the collective consciousness of our humanness. Sacred wisdom is contained in the connection to your spirit, and using music to remember how to develop and maintain this connection is the focus of this book.

We begin walking a spiritual path when we cultivate a connection with our spirit. The connection begins when we are ready to listen. Our spirit has always been speaking to us. It has a job to do while we are here and would love for us to hear the messages it has been giving us. Cultivating this connection is simple, and we have powerful tools such as music to help us. Listening requires us to be silent. We cannot listen and speak at the same time. So it is also the case that we cannot listen to our spirit and think at the same time. We need to stop thinking for just a moment and allow the voice of our spirit to be heard. Music is excellent for this and can naturally provide the space and time needed for us to cultivate a deep connection with our spirit. So, stop everything and either listen to music or play a musical instrument, talk to your spirit and be ready to receive the guidance that only your inner being can give you.

The connection to our Spirit creates a new paradigm of self-realization that places our perceptions in alignment with our spiritual being. Finding our path is simple and we can begin or continue walking at any moment. There is no need to wait for something to happen or for you to fulfill a pre-requisite. You do not need to attend a school, get certified or reach a place of distinguished standing. The spiritual path is one of passion, experience and adventure. It is not an intellectual or academic venture.

Finding your spiritual path requires only one thing: a sincere desire to connect to the sacred wisdom and the Divine inside you. Once the desire is sincere and you are ready to surrender to it, the universe will conspire with you to create the life you want. You will feel inspired and have the tools to manifest your dreams into your reality. You will begin to notice how the universe conspires with you to create everything you need to evolve to higher levels of awareness, and life will become a great adventure filled with magic, contentment and inner peace.

The opportunity to begin walking a deeper path is here. Every moment offers you the possibility of transformation. It doesn't to take a long time. Transformation can occur in an instant. At the same time, we must have the patience to wait and the passion to feel uncomfortable, and we must lose the desire for instant gratification. Because of the inability to reconcile this, we will often wait to make changes until it is imperative or until some kind of trauma has occurred, forcing us to implement changes or suffer further consequences.

In 2000, I was working very hard at developing my business. I had been teaching percussion and bringing teachers from West Africa to town to teach, as well as playing many performances. I was burning the candle at both ends, as they say. In September of that year, I invested $5,000 in bringing one of my teachers to town. It was a significant financial risk and I wasn't sure if I would break even. I worked very hard at getting the word out, and when the weekend came around, it turned out to be a success. It was the only workshop I produced that actually produced a profit for myself. I was happy but exhausted.

When the weekend was over, I began thinking that I wanted to make some changes in my life. I reflected on how I had been thinking about this for many months but had not allowed myself to bring it to the front of my thoughts. I was very good at compartmentalizing my emotions, especially those that carried feelings of guilt or shame. Self-inflected suffering was always the most uncomfortable for me, and I would often ignore those feelings and just want them to go away. I thought the reason I could not make any changes was that I was moving so fast; my life was a runaway train. It seemed to be running faster than I could keep up with it. Or, at least that is what I convinced myself of at the time. Regardless, when you sincerely ask the universe, your higher self, your inner being, God, or whatever you choose to call the Divine to intervene in your life, know that you will receive that intervention. It may not look like what you thought you were asking for, or it may look exactly like what you asked for. Be careful, my friends—ask and you shall receive.

One afternoon, I was sitting on my back porch and began to cry in frustration that I could not make any changes while life was moving so fast. I got down on my knees and told anyone listening that I wanted life to stop for a while. I said aloud. "I want my life to stop for two weeks so that I can make some changes, become healthier and learn how to slow down, enjoy life and learn to be happy." The crying faded and I got up and went through the rest of my day. The next day was a busy one for me. I played two outdoor performances and played another one that evening that I had put together, promoted and managed. I got through the day on cigarettes and coffee.

That evening I went to bed feeling a bit sick but not bad enough to pay attention to it, let alone mention to anyone. I awoke at 1:10 a.m. looking down at my body lying on the bed. I was near the ceiling. It took a moment for me to realize that I was not in my body but floating above it. It was then that I heard a voice. It told me I had a choice to make. I could continue upward, away from my body, or I could go back into it. It was an easy choice at first, based on the feeling I had when I thought about continuing away from my body. The feeling was euphoric, blissful. It was what I had been looking for, happiness, joy and deep contentment. Then I looked back down at my body, I thought of my family and my close friends and I felt sadness, their sadness. But I had a realization that changed my perception. I had a memory of agreeing to come to Earth for a specific reason. I remembered the agreement I had made before coming into this body and I realized that I had not finished what I had agreed to do while on Earth. I couldn't leave now; it was not time.

I slowly made it back into my body, and as I became conscious of being in my body, well, that is when the chaos began. I awoke and began vomiting. I was sick beyond what my mind could imagine. Eventually, I managed to sleep and woke up the next day feeling better, I thought. As the morning went on, I had no appetite and did not eat. Very soon, it became apparent that I was sicker than I had realized, because I could not keep water down. I vomited every time I put something into my stomach. Soon, things went from bad to worse and I was urinating and vomiting blood. The doctors at the hospital were very confused by my condition. Both kidneys had stopped. The diagnosis was full renal failure. They could not figure out how a generally healthy 30-year-old person with no history of kidney problems and no hereditary tendencies could have double renal failure. They called in specialists, but no one could understand.

I rejected the morphine the wanted to give me to relieve the pain of excess water between my organs and my skin. I knew I had to be in my body and present for this experience and to receive the messages waiting for me along the way. I had dreams of other worlds where beings dreamed things into existence and transformed things with love. I danced with fear and fell in love with loneliness, shame and humiliation, so that each of them melted into nothingness. I felt connected to the universal life force that we all are, and I finally surrendered to death. In that surrender, I played music and sang with death. I engaged in a delicate dance to balance the resistance to suffering and death inside my being. Death became a mirror in which I saw my reflection, in which I saw the immortal, and I was free.

Death challenges us from the moment we are born into this earthly world. Sister Death waits patiently for us to recognize her, to honor her and to dance with her. For many, death is silent and never spoken of. She is the unwelcome guest who is ignored for fear that acknowledging her will bring her closer. Being close to Sister Death is undesirable for those who live with a fear of death. It is only when we have taken the hand of Sister Death, honored her, eaten and danced with her that we can experience the freedom that life offers us.

There are physical and metaphorical types of death, and Sister Death offers us so much in the form of spiritual growth and transformation. She offers us the opportunity to dance with life in a way that changes our perception and expands and heightens our awareness. By having a deep respect and honor for Sister Death and her role in the universe, we can maintain a balance of energy, serenity and inner peace.

Within three days, my kidneys were back to full function, and the doctors reluctantly released me. I promised to return for weekly checkups, but there were no further complications. The doctors never did understand what had happened, but I had. The first lesson was, be careful what you ask for—you may just receive it. The second lesson was, be brave to be free, relax to be happy and have an open heart to receive guidance and messages. We hear about having an open heart, but I think we do not fully comprehend what that means. It is a perception that embodies a perspective of the world and the universe we live in. What does it feel like? For me, it is a vibration in my heart chakra, or heart center, like a motor running. A burning sensation. The practice for cultivating an open heart is not difficult. It consists of a simple, yet powerful vision of surrendering to death, being willing to die today, right now, being willing to leave this planet, surrendering to Spirit with unconditional love and humility. Make some time on a regular basis to cultivate this vision. Open your heart, expand your perception and strengthen your relationship with life.

After that experience and with direction from guides, both physical and spiritual, I began to make changes. I learned how to relax, slow down and enjoy each moment. I began to eat more slowly. I learned how to allow my spiritual and energetic being to be more present and how to be clear in my awareness. I began to meditate and loved to listen to music while meditating. I picked music that embodied the energy of expansion. I began to experience the power of music in meditation and the ability of music and sound to be a vessel for energy.

I began to remember that I am more than my body and that I can engage the invisible aspect of me to travel to other places in the universe. This came to me as a complete memory; I had sensory and physical sensations of being out of this body and in other locations or dimensions.

Some years ago, I awoke around one o'clock in the morning and felt inspired to meditate. I rose from my bed and went to the living room, sat on my couch and put on a pair of headphones. At that time, I was experiencing an energy practice that consisted of engaging a complete surrender to Universal Life-Force Energy. My mission was to forget who I think I am and what I think I know, to know that I am more than my body and connected to the Energy of All Life.

I often practiced my relaxation session with one or more recordings of a series of guided meditations. The recording was infused with powerful energy called "supercreative life-force energy". Whenever I listened to those guided meditations, I felt my heart chakra open, and each time I listened, it opened even more.

This time I felt my heart open so wide that I had to regulate my breathing so I could stay with it. It pushed my comfort zone and I was on the verge of thinking that my heart could stop at any moment. I felt fear coming upon my being, but instead of owning that fear, I surrendered to it. I decided in that moment that if it was my time to die, I was willing. Honestly, I thought this would be an excellent way to die, to feel such an overwhelming sense of euphoria that I could just go with it. Within seconds of surrendering, I felt and saw myself lift from my body. I was now hovering just above my head, and then I was near the ceiling of my living room. It was then that I noticed a force greater than me pulling me toward the heavens. I began to fly upward, through the ceiling and above the house. I could see everything, the trees, my neighbors' homes, the lights of the neighborhood. As I continued to rise, I could see the lights of the city, and then, as I flew higher, I could see the lights of surrounding cities, and soon the lights of all of North America came into view. I can remember resisting the anxiety that wanted to engulf me; I had to keep surrendering to death. I thought that if I allowed anxiety and fear to consume me, the experience would end and I would not be in a position to receive whatever I was supposed to receive that night. I kept going, and before too long I looked up to the sky and saw the most beautiful scene I had ever seen.

I was now among the stars, the planets and the galaxies. I had left the Milky Way and was on a path to the brightest star, beyond what I could have ever imagined. I soon felt as if I was moving toward the star and then realized that I was being pulled into it. I looked down at my chest and saw it open; there seemed to be a slit in the middle. Two flaps opened and exposed a ball of light inside me. I looked toward the bright star I was moving toward. There was a beam of light coming from the star and going directly into my chest. It was giving me life, a kind of energy I had never felt before. It was beautiful, and the feeling it produced in me is beyond any words I can say or write. Telling you that it was euphoric is minimizing it tremendously. It was beyond any sensation I had ever felt, and I knew it was a part of something very powerful. I felt so small and so alive at the same time. It was then that I looked around and realized I was not alone. I was surrounded by hundreds, maybe thousands, of other beings, some human, some not human. We are all attached by beams of light and connected to this beautiful source of life-force energy.

We spent years there, attached to this star. We remembered and experienced compassion, humility, forgiveness and love. We remembered how connected we all are and that when one of us suffers, we all suffer. We remembered how important it is to set aside our ambitions, wants and desires and develop a desire to be of service. We remembered that our individual needs were an illusion and that we would receive everything we wanted and more if we could let go and surrender to helping the group evolve. We had experiences in spiritual alchemy and learned how to transform resistance into nonresistance and fear into love. Most of all, we remembered how to open our hearts in a way we never thought possible, and we remembered that all things are created from love.

Love is our most powerful asset for creating and manifesting positive change in the spiritual and physical realms. Cultivating an open heart, both physically and spiritually, will create opportunities to experience unconditional love. Ultimately, having an open heart means having a deep sense of unconditional love for all beings and our home, Mother Earth. Having an open heart manifests in the physical world as acts of kindness, gratitude, compassion, forgiveness, humility and unconditional love. Having an open heart requires us to access the sacred wisdom of our inner beings to cultivate pure intentions with our thoughts and actions.

With this open heart we continue walking with patience, detachment from negativity and honor for our inner being and for those who guide us. Walking this path requires that we implement a set of virtues and values that honor the Divinity inside each of us and in those who have walked before us. We should recognize the value of cultivating this connection to our Spirit and make it the highest priority on a daily basis. We should honor the Masters who have come before us and serve to show us the path to our inner beings. The more time we spend with our Spirit, the more intimate we become with it, the more valuable it becomes to us and the higher we prioritize it in our life.

What Is Healing?

For many, a spiritual path evokes the idea of healing the physical, mental, emotional and spiritual bodies. What is healing, and is it necessary for walking a deep spiritual path? In walking a spiritual path, I recognize that healing is the process of melting with Universal life-force energy. It is the alignment of mind, body and spirit. Humans have a Spiritual, Mental, Emotional, and Physical body. All bodies can be healed, some as a byproduct of healing others. For example, the emotional body will heal when we focus our energy on healing the spiritual body.

The emotional body affects the mind and visa versa. Negative emotions produce negative thoughts, and if we choose to engage them, they can produce negative actions, which, in turn, often have negative and unproductive consequences. Healing the emotional body will often heal the mind and, in positive ways, transform the way we think.

The mind will reproduce and project whatever it constructs. If the mind constructs a reality full of stress, anxiety and fear, it will reproduce this and project it onto our daily experiences. If the mind constructs a reality of compassion, gratitude and inner peace, it will reproduce this, and our perception will transform accordingly. It is up to us to produce healthy mental constructs that create an environment in which the mind can develop positive thoughts and perceptions. So many of us developed negative landscapes of the mind during our youth and carried them into adulthood. They have permeated our perceptions and are the foundation of our unhappiness and discontent with the world around us. Yes, our own perceptions are the source of our suffering. The world around is as it is, and it is up to us to adapt and alter our perceptions to change our position in relation to it. It will not change simply because we do not enjoy it or because we think it causes us discomfort.

Changing our perceptions and creating a nurturing environment in which the mind can cultivate positive perceptions is very simple but not always easy. The mind will always want to fight, to defend itself endlessly and evaluate everything and create judgments based on those evaluations. You can make it a practice to stop fighting, stop judging, be silent and listen. Your Spirit contains a very important element necessary for creating your reality: peace. The Spirit knows that there is no peace in opposition of any kind. When you oppose something, anything, you are out of peace. There is no possibility for peace when you are in opposition, because opposition does not reside in peace. If you want inner peace, choose to let go of resistance and judgment. Practice acceptance every day and one day you will see that you are in peace, happy and content. Then you will be in an optimum position to transform and change the world for the better.

Sometimes we need to begin with smaller steps before we can remember to stop judging or fighting. Sometimes we need to be reminded that we are capable of anything, that we are worth the effort and that what we hear in our thoughts may not be our own words. Negative messages tell us that we are not good enough, not smart enough, incapable, and unworthy. Here I am reminded that the mind produces more of what it hears. There are ways to change the old messages and create new ones that offer opportunity in the adventures of life. Creating new and positive messages requires us to rewrite the script and begin walking toward our destiny. My own story illustrates this experience.

When I was young I had a difficult relationship with my father. In many ways, we were very much alike. We both had very strong opinions, and they were often at the opposite ends of the spectrum. At times, we argued and said unkind words to each other. One day, when I was a teenager, I heard my father's voice in my head. It was saying some of the unkind things he had said to me in the past. I stopped what I was doing and became terrified that my fathers voice was in my head. I thought about how insidious it was that my mind had adopted what it had been told by someone outside of my being and now it was repeating those words on its own and without my permission. I was horrified at the realization at that moment that my mind did not belong to me. I felt a sense of desperation at the realization that it did not belong to anyone and was looking for someone to give it direction. Fortunately, I was able to step outside my thoughts and observe the phenomena of what was taking place,; and I realized that I had to step up and take charge of the situation inside my head, or my father's voice was going to become my own voice and take control of my thoughts, my perceptions and my life.

I scrambled for something to combat this invasion of negative, character-degrading thoughts. As I often did, I played my drum set for reflection. As I played I realized something. What came to me was so simple, a piece of wisdom from the Master within my inner being. I realized that if my mind would accept foreign input as legitimate, it would surely accept my own input as legitimate as well. I thought that if I could enter more positive input than any negative that was already in there, the positive would outweigh the negative and win the battle. The negative would die, and no one else's voice could ever determine my perceptions, thoughts or the outcome of my life. That moment changed my life. I got up from my drum set and walked to my bathroom. I looked into the mirror and told myself that I was not all those negative things the voice said I was. I told myself I was too young to deserve the responsibility of anyone's unhappiness beyond myself. I told myself that I was inherently a good person and that I could do anything and be anyone I wanted, that I could accomplish anything I set out to do and become who I wanted to be, without influence from anyone else. I demanded that my mind stay loyal to me alone and reject the cruel words of others. I set an intention to forgive my father for his unkind words, as I realized that he had not intended for them to be stored and replayed inside my mind.

I continued the practice of talking to myself in front of the mirror for a year or so, until I sensed that the voice was gone and would never return. Initially, it was uncomfortable and I felt strange looking into my own eyes and talking out loud to myself in the mirror. I was concerned that my family would hear me and think I was not well in some way. Regardless, I knew I had to do it if I wanted to live without these outside thoughts. It became easier over time. I reflected more about the fact that my father's words had become embedded in my mind and played like a recording throughout the day and night. I thought about how my grandfather must have said unkind and cruel things to my father and how those statements were now being handed down to me like a gift from one generation to another. I consider this a gift because I did not ask for it. This gift was not an attractive one; it wasn't wrapped in nice paper or decorated with a ribbon. Nor was it given with the recognition that a gift usually comes with, no card with a nice message written on it. This kind of gift is often given in disguise so that the receiver doesn't even know he is being given the gift. It is like bacteria that enters the body and goes undetected until it has grown into something that cannot be destroyed. People offer us gifts every day, some healthy and beautiful and some unhealthy and destructive.

I knew that I did not have to accept this gift and that I could end the cycle of shame that had been handed down from generation to generation for so many years. That practice helped me feel more comfortable with myself, gave me tools to help with emotional healing, and empowered me to take charge of my destiny. In addition, it helped me realize the power of intention, and of the Spirit and the mind. Until we remember the power of our Spirit, the mind will lead us. When the Spirit leads the way, the mind will follow.

We can apply the message of that story to all the virtues we need on a spiritual path. We can infuse our thoughts with gratitude, compassion, forgiveness, humility and unconditional love, and the more we practice integrating them into our daily lives, the less possibility there will be for negative emotions to exist within us. Ultimately, we are able to entertain the notion that negative and unproductive emotions will no longer exist within us. They are unproductive because they distract us from our spiritual path. Negative emotions need to be fed. They are hungry for attention and require energy to stay alive within us. The more we focus on infusing our thoughts with positive virtues such as forgiveness, compassion, humility, and unconditional love, the less food there is for negative emotions. When we master this practice, we will no longer be vulnerable to negative emotions, and we will be in a position to teach others through our actions. This is a powerful way to be of service to the awakening of the planet.

While it may take a person a lifetime or many lifetimes to be a Master of Contentment, developing the inner wisdom of unconditional love can begin now. Cultivating unconditional love for all beings will create an expansion of your consciousness. It will open your perceptions to a kind of freedom you thought was possible only in fairy tales, a kind of freedom that allows you to connect to everything in the deepest way possible for human beings. In the West, we have been taught that one cannot love others unless one loves oneself first. I want to reverse this idea and suggest that the opposite is true. One learns how to love oneself through giving unconditional love to others. What I mean is that we always receive exactly what we need when we are in service to others. When we love unconditionally, we are a vessel for divine energy, which purifies and heals the vessel.

◩   ◩   ◩

A New Paradigm of Love and Healing

I think the real issue here lies in our definition of love. Words are symbols that are connected to ideas, which often dictate how we choose to think, feel or behave. A large part of changing our perceptions to experience more freedom relies on our ability to redefine words we have taken for granted. Love is a word that represents one of the most important ideas in life and the universe. We know that all things are created with love, yet we have been able to deconstruct the idea of love and reconstruct it to fit into a belief system that is based on a cause and effect and fear-based reality.

We need to redefine love and begin to accept nothing short of unconditional and unlimited love. The definition of love that we use in this culture is laced with unrelated ideas that have nothing to do with unconditional and unlimited love. For example, how many of us have been in relationships with people we were "in love" with until they cheated or betrayed us in some way. Then our love quickly disappeared and we retreated into fear-based protectionism. Our feelings of betrayal dictated that we no longer extended love to our partners, and some of us responded to the offense with criticisms and hurtful words. We no longer allowed them into our hearts and refrained from extending "love" to them.

Unconditional and Unlimited Love does not discriminate between those who are kind to us and those who hurt us. It does not restrict access until your partner has changed to accommodate your desires. Unconditional and Unlimited Love accepts everyone as he is, right now. Love is unconditional – always. The love that we are accustomed to is not unconditional or unlimited. We have given love a very shallow definition within the parameters of romantic relationships. This is romance, and romantic love that we have twisted and shaped in attempts to protect us from our own fear of separateness. This is not love; this is an illusion of love, a projection of what we would like to see and experience, a perfect fantasy until it is shattered. Then it becomes a tragedy, where the mind takes us on a self-inflicted journey of suffering. There is wisdom in that journey if we choose to take it. Otherwise, we can skip it by choosing unconditional love, where we have nothing to protect, where in loving others we receive all the self-love available to us.

The same is true for healing. When we are sincere in wanting to help others heal, we become a vehicle for spirit. Whenever we allow spirit to move through us, we are getting the healing that we need. It is a natural byproduct of being a vessel for spirit to heal others. Set the intention to heal others and you will be healed. Love others and you will be loved.

The physical body can be healed when conditions are favorable. The decision to heal is made in the spirit world by our spirits, guides and masters. Through ceremony, we can access energies that can transform and rearrange this physical world. I receive many calls from people asking for a healing. They have some discomfort they would like to see disappear and are hoping I can remove the discomfort for them. I am not in the business of healing; I am negotiating for balance. I am dancing, and the movement of dance requires space, so I am making space for new energy to replace the old and stagnant energy. If it is the intention of the person seeking the healing to let go of the old messages and create a new paradigm for the new energy to exist within him, then it can occur. I can only ask for an opening and help create the possibility of healing. Often we heal ourselves without knowing it and just need someone to validate that healing. Other times we need permission to let go and move on to write the next chapter of life. I am a facilitator and manager of energy for those wanting to grow and transform with unconditional love, gratitude, forgiveness and humility.

Spiritual healing is different for everyone and may be defined in relation to the person's belief system. Some people believe that living a full life consists of a full range of emotions, positive and negative, and experiencing the full range makes them feel alive. For those people, healing simply means finding a balance of emotions in everyday life; to deny these people the full range of emotions would not be respectful, productive or healing. To others, spiritual healing may mean the eradication of negative emotions. These people have a belief system that allows them to fully eliminate any negative emotional experience. They recognize that negative emotions exist whether they identify with them or not. They choose to detach from any negative emotional experience and remain in a place of inner peace in every moment. They are immune to inner chaos and confusion and maintain a connection with inner wisdom at all times. These individuals are enlightened.

Enlightenment is something that many of us have heard of, especially if we have read anything regarding Buddhism or the Buddha; but how many of us know someone who is enlightened? In modern society, Enlightenment seems to be a thing of the past, something that the ancients had access to but is now unavailable or unreachable. Enlightenment, or being "with the light," is a perception and a heightened and expanded state of awareness. It is a continual practice of detachment that requires passion to create a deep devotional position of detachment, gratitude, forgiveness, compassion, humility, serenity and unconditional love. It is available to all of us. The mystics of all religions offer us the opportunity to experience enlightenment, and all of them offer us similar wisdom in pursuing it. They tell us that enlightenment is not something we can possess, buy, sell, own or contain. It is not something that, once we have, we will always have. Enlightenment is always moving, transforming and changing; it is available to those who are willing to surrender to the art of life, death and love.

I believe that it is possible to participate in enlightenment in this lifetime and that music is our ticket to the performance that is playing now. We are already inside the performance hall, and it is time for our part in the play. How will we write our script, our story, and how will we act it out?

CHAPTER TWO

Music Is Medicine

*"Music is a higher revelation
than all wisdom or philosophy"*
- Beethoven

Cosmic Sound

Sound is at the creation of the universe through cosmic vibrations, and galaxies are thought to be created from particular vibrations. Everything we know of resonates at a particular vibration, rate, and frequency, and science has confirmed that at an atomic level, the sound of cosmic vibrations is at the heart of everything. All things oscillate at specific rates, and the power of sound can indeed be used to manipulate the oscillation of atomic particles, which creates a transformation in the physical world. Music gives credence to activities that ancient cultures thought impossible. Given what we know regarding sound's ability to alter the nonphysical vibratory aspects of all objects, it is a valid possibility that monumental events such as the construction of ancient temples such as Stonehenge, the great pyramids of Egypt, the stone-hewn churches of Ethiopia and the sacred stone temples in South America and Mexico were created with sound and music.

Knowledge of the power of sound and music is reflected in the creation stories of ancient cultures around the world. Most cultures around the world have a creation stories that includes the cosmic vibrations of music and sound, and most of these stories contain the idea that an omnipotent being created Mother Earth with sound, music and dance and that sound and music were given to humans by God or the gods. The cosmic vibrations of music are used to disclose God's will and impart to humans the deepest secrets of God's will. In this way, music is living communication. As R.J. Stewart stated in his 1980 book The Spiritual Dimension of Music, "Music may one day provide us a path of communication with states of awareness or self-aware beings that we cannot at present comprehend." Music is a powerful technology and humans have been using it to communicate with self-aware beings for thousands of years. Indigenous cultures around the world have been living this reality just as long. We in the West have been disconnected from this reality for so long that we have forgotten the power of music to connect us to the universe and all it offers us, including communication with other beings in other dimensions. Stewart was absolutely correct in that he predicted that we will again remember who we are and re-connect with the ancient technology of music.

Our cosmic memory also offers us the realization that music offers us a map of the universe. When a sound is produced, it is always a combination of sounds. What we call a note is actually a combination of sounds or harmonics that create a unified sound. These harmonics hold the key to the universe. They offer us direct connection to the subtle energies of other dimensions and the beings that exist there.

Music engages our cosmic memory and allows us to connect with these spirits and the specific areas of the universe where they reside. It reveals a hidden map to the reaches of the universe and beyond what the eye can see. Music opens doors to other dimensions and offers us access to the knowledge and wisdom contained there. Music is also our interpreter when we travel to these dimensions. Our mind is not equipped to translate the message waiting for us there, but music is a language that is bidirectional. We can use it to communicate and receive the messages the mind cannot perceive. Music opens pathways to and from our spirit center, or our inner being. Our inner being does not use the mind; rather, it uses energy to gain knowledge and information. Music provides the information highway from our inner being to the universal life-force consciousness that contains all we need to evolve. This is not an external highway; it does not lead us outside ourselves. Rather, it leads us deeper inside our being, to a collective consciousness where we all exist together, complete, pure and one.

Music is a manifestation of an inner sound, a cosmic sound, that exists inside each of us. This inner sound reflects cosmic vibrations and connects us to the universe and each other. Here we must differentiate between audible sound and cosmic sound. All people can hear audible sounds, whereas cosmic sound can be heard by those who practice deep levels of detachment and transform their perceptions of the mundane world – by those who can see and hear beyond the veil of the material, those who see with inner eyes and hear with inner ears. Audible sound is a reflection of cosmic vibrations or sound—the source of all life.

Historically, these cosmic vibrations are reflected as Mantras in spiritual traditions throughout the world. Mantras are words that hold cosmic power and are a reflection of divine cosmic sound. The word Mantra comes from the Sanskrit language and can be translated as "thoughts that liberate from samsara (the world of illusions)." Mantras can be a single syllable or a combination of words and are most commonly recited to achieve higher states of consciousness and alignment with divine cosmic energy.

All indigenous peoples and all religions have at least one Mantra. According to the Vedas, ancient Hindu scripts, the sacred sound of "om" is the source of all creation and the source of all living things. The universe is created and maintained through the sacred sound of "om". The Sufi tradition uses "hu" and Tibetan Buddhists use "ah". Most cultures also have instruments that reflect this sacred vibration. The Sufi blow the Nai, a double flute, Hindu Yogis blow the Singh, a horn. The Aztecs blow the Tēcciztli, or conch shell. And Tibetan monks blow the Rag-Dung, or ceremonial horn. I write about this here to illustrate the point that the notion that sound holds the most important function of cosmic creation is a long-standing idea that has crossed cultures, geographic space and linear time. There are many books written on this specific topic, and since going beyond the above information is not central to this book, I will not go further with it here.

◙   ◙   ◙

The Power of Music to Heal and Transform

Music is an essential part of life and a force that can create transformation inside the individual, the community and the world. Music is the intentional use of sound and silence and offers us the possibility to experience the spiritual physically and the physical spiritually. It is a bridge between space and time. As humans, we can access the dimension of time, and this allows us the opportunity to use music to access other dimensions. For example, the folkloric and traditional lullabies of every culture give agency to the notion of the dream time and our existence in other dimensions. Many of us can remember the kind of dreams we had when the voice of the lullaby escorted us to other realms. The music soothed our soul and healed our hearts; we interacted with other beings, received messages and brought back a sense of comfort to the physical world.

Sound waves are vehicles of energy capable of carrying more than just sound. We can infuse sound with our intentions of gratitude, compassion, forgiveness, humility and unconditional love. These are powerful tools that can heal and transform. This is sound with a soul! Music provides us a vehicle for the manifestation of cosmic sound. Playing music within this sacred context is a powerful spiritual tool, and infusing sound with pure intentions offers us the possibility of connecting to the divine inside each of us. Music played in collaboration with pure intention can create a potent recipe for inner transformation. Music has the power to move us out of negative emotional states and into places of opportunity and possibility.

All of us are seeking healing, whether physical, emotional, mental or spiritual, and music plays an important part in that healing; it allows us to move into the spirit world, where healing occurs. Music affects the body directly through cells and organs and indirectly through emotions, which, in turn, also affects the cells and organs. Music can affect our energy, our nervous system and our digestion. Music can add to our clarity of consciousness and strengthen our life-force energy. These functions of music allow for us to co-create a powerful message of healing. When we set the intention to participate in healing, we transport ourselves to the space of the immortal—the dimensions of immortality. This is where the message of healing is created. We can use music combined with our pure intention to deliver the message back to the physical world. Intention combined with music is a powerful connection to our Spirit, and intention comes from the core of who you are, beyond the mind. Intentions are actions in the unseen world and create powerful results when combined with music. They transform energy and can manifest transformation in the physical realm if that is what is needed. Our most powerful and productive intention originates from the heart, which is connected to our Spirit.

Listening to music connects our perception to open streams of consciousness that provide possibilities of freedom and self-realization. Negative emotional states are closed and caged states of consciousness. Music combined with sincere intention opens these closed states and creates an open flow, allowing our perceptions to create a path to emotional freedom. In this way, music helps us break free of old patterns and unwanted habits.

Music is a perfect cocktail of innocence, playfulness and wisdom. Music knows when to speak and when to remain silent. Music knows when to say something reverent and when to speak of tall tales and folly. Music knows what is productive and unproductive for us to engage. Music asks, "Who am I?" Ask the music and be open to receive the answer. Music reveals a path to the divine, a place deep inside us where spoken language cannot enter. The door is unlocked by music. It offers us permission to enter this sacred space and to partake in the fruits of music. It is like eating pure, unlimited love and creating life with our breath. Music enables us to live like the gods, with sincerity, humility and responsibility. We offer everything our spirits have to music, and in return music offers her life back to us in the form of freedom.

The petals of the flowers tremble silently as the strings of the harp are played for the little ones. Just arriving, they are fresh and scared. The music soothes their spirit as they wait for guidance. Finally the directions are given and the little ones scurry off to their new home in music. Music is the best place to be, the most cherished place for little ones to serve, and how they serve is not questioned or even talked about. They know the power of music and they know that to speak of it might limit its potential to heal the universe. The little ones reside in every note the healer plays, chants, and sings. They are the catalyst for transformation. The little ones are divine love.

Music and love are brother and sister. Music resides in the seen and the unseen simultaneously. Love resides in everything. Music and love share the same breath, and they are of the same mother and father. When we play music we are in love. We gain the awareness of love, and love knows no boundaries or limits. When we see the world and others through the lens of music, we cease to exist in the way we did in the past. We are new, authentic and pure. Music provides us a mirror to see who we are and reflect on how we are in relationship in the world. How is music like your life? This question will provide you the answers to your other questions about what needs to change in your life. Do you struggle with particular rhythms but cannot muster the discipline to change them? Is everything fine until it is time to change or transition to another part, phrase or chapter in your life? Music offers us insight into how we are negotiating the lessons life offers us. It asks us to look at our life and reflect on what we can do to transform into the beings we agreed to be in this lifetime.

Music teaches us to be in the present moment. Here, now—it is all we have and contains the past and future. Music asks us to fully commit to her whenever we engage her loving arms. Music teaches us to view our world with invisible eyes and hear with invisible ears. She demands that we speak in poetry rather than linear words. Music holds a mirror to our perception of self and others and asks that we see through a lens of clarity. Music asks bold action in life and requests that we take risks, stopping at nothing for freedom and love. Music teaches us that we are always in relationship and shows us that we are connected to others. Music is the action of the heart; it informs our thoughts and teaches us how to communicate with intention and meaning.

Our beliefs are predicated on experience, either direct experience or vicarious experienced gained through others' stories or teachings. Music gives us direct knowledge of all that is. Music makes no judgments, assumptions or assertions. Music is neutral and always reflects our intentions, thoughts and beliefs. Music acts like a mirror and reflects back to us the perceptions of our being. Music teaches us to stay objective, practice detachment and manage our energy wisely. Music exists in the now and requires that we also be in the present moment. Music teaches us that there is no other place to be and nowhere to go. When we play music, we are completely in the present moment, the now. This is where everything happens; the past, future and present all exist in the now. Music provides us access to all that the now offers.

Playing Music for Inner Transformation

Music is a vehicle for the messages that the whole person needs to evolve spiritually. That message comes from the universe, the place that resides deep within our spirit and is mirrored in every galaxy and star system beyond our imagination. Play music and you are in love. How can one play music and be in conflict? Music is a perfect balance between the sound and the silence. How can this balance create conflict internally? When we play music, we are creating a bridge over any troubles we may think we have, and certainly we transcend any internal conflict we struggle with. Music offers us permission to leave the troubles behind, for good. Music does not say, "Just for now you may be peaceful, but later you may struggle". Music tells us that we may always have the peace we have when we are playing music. That inner peace is with us always; it is up to us to recognize and engage it. Peace waits patiently, and eternally. Music reminds us of who we are; it tempts us to remember our cosmic memory of many lifetimes. Music burns away the layers of struggle and leads us to an inner sanctuary. Forget any struggle, for there is no struggle. Play music and enjoy life; there is nothing more to do.

Playing music transforms our faculties of perception and enables us to expand our parameters. Music allows our peripheral perceptions to become more visible, and we are able to see through the veil of the material world into the depths of the spiritual worlds. Music is an elixir for the mind; it allows the mind to drop its protective layers and expose what resides deep inside itself. Yes, music can reveal what resides inside the mind. Music is the lullaby that allows the mind to let down its protective barrier just long enough that we may enter into the nucleus. It soothes the mind and coaxes it into relaxing and revealing its vulnerability. Then it slowly dismantles the mind, like picking the petals from a flower to reveal the innermost center. What is revealed is beautiful and vulnerable. For so long we have been saying this is a process of no-mind. Now it is a process of melting with what is at the nucleus: nothing, emptiness. It has all been a great façade, the mind creating one illusion after another, like the Wizard of Oz being just a little man behind the curtain, manipulating the controls. We should never underestimate the power of music!

I can remember when I first began playing the drum with the intention of expanding my awareness and deepening my own spiritual connection. Initially, I had to undo some training I had developed around the drum. I came from a background of being trained to play specific parts in a specific way. My mind was deeply involved in making sure I was playing "correctly" and abiding by the rules I had learned regarding playing technique, posture, rhythmic sensibility and timing. I came to realize that these were all assets if I could learn to let go of the mind and further develop my faculties of intuition and intention. As I sat with the drum, I began to play not what I had learned in a class or workshop but what Spirit wanted me to play. I began a process of no thinking and no judgment about what came through my being, into my hands and out the drum. I found that I was able to utilize all the training I had gotten from initiated masters of the djembe, and I did not have to think about any of that. I had learned the language of the djembe well enough that I could allow my inner being to speak an ancient language of music and lead the way to the spirit realms.

After some time, the experiences I had were magical, and the physical sensations were euphoric and ecstatic. Thankfully, I was aware of the trickery of the mind in interpreting these sensations. If I weren't careful, it would have been easy for me to consider these sensations to be the goal of the experience. We should always remember that any sensations we experience associated with our participation in the spiritual realms are not the goal of our experience; they are byproducts of being a human being with a nervous system. The human experience embodies sensations, and while they may be valuable in our existence in the physical world, they are merely sensations and having them should not be taken as reaching a deep spiritual place. That being said, I did recognize them as markers of being on the right track. Pleasant sensations such as euphoria are often felt when we connect to our spirit and allow it to guide us as we navigate multiple realities and dimensions.

What came out of those drumming sessions with Spirit was a beautiful connection with the divine. I had developed a powerful tool for deepening my spiritual path. As I continued to use the drum to access the sacred wisdom of my inner being, I began to perceive my life from a much deeper and wiser place. My perceptions began to change; I began to make decisions that held my desire of a spiritual path as my highest priority. I began to close doors that did not serve this goal. I observed how acting on these decisions did not affect me like I thought they would. I was receiving more wisdom and felt more at peace inside, with an inner knowing that more was waiting for me as soon as I surrendered to the messages and took action.

Music teaches us about life and how to be in it. Music can help us define and refine our relationships to others, Mother Earth and ourselves. When we play music with others, we are in a committed relationship. We are committed to participation in the language of music with another human being at that moment. We are completely engaged in that relationship and offer everything we have to support it. We are givers and receive everything that giving offers in return. The language of music originates in the heart and is spoken with sacred intention. Since music places us in the present moment, originates from the heart and is spoken with sacred intention, it offers us the precious opportunity to share in the magic of life, which is love. Music is love. When we play music, we are offered the possibility to see the world from a perspective of unity, love and serenity.

Music is a matter of our perception. Music is a language, and like all languages, it is a product of our perception and it also helps us create our perception. Music exists for us to perceive and create reality in just the way we need to use it. When we use the power of our energy, intention and the language of music, we create a potent combination suitable for healing, for love. Music is love. Melt with music and be love. Be music and melt with love.

⊡   ⊡   ⊡

The Healing Sound

The way the language of music interacts with our body is unique. Music is a powerful infusion of energy, intention and sound. It can be used to open the energy centers of our body and allow for a larger capacity to contain and manage energy. The energy that music uses or the frequencies that music resides in are the same frequencies stored in our energy centers, or chakras. The chakras help us receive, regulate and use energy. A combination of music, energy and intention can be arranged and sequenced so that it may aid in clearing and opening our chakras. It can also be a powerful way to keep our whole being healthy, clear and aware. Clearing our energy centers provides a foundation for clarity on physical, mental, emotional and spiritual levels. This is commonly known as "sound healing".

Sound healing has become popular in the West with the use of crystal bowls that resonate at particular frequencies. These frequencies match others that modern science recognizes in and around the body. Sound healing with crystal bowls is a good example of how science has touched the perimeter of a spiritual phenomenon. Whether singing, chanting or making sounds with physical materials, humans have been manipulating and transforming energy with sound for thousands of years.

Music of the Illuminated

The spiritual musician is responsible for transmitting the message in every situation every time he plays music. The musician is a mediator between our humanness and our Divinity. He helps remind us who we are. We are humans with one foot in the physical and one foot in the spiritual. We are spiritual beings having human experiences, and music connects those experiences back to the spiritual, creating and completing a circle of life and love.

When the hands of the illuminated play music, it will bring all peoples into an age of peace and unity. The spiritual musician plays with his heart and the listener listens with his heart. Spiritual music is a stream of consciousness that reflects the inner state of the spiritual musician. The spiritual musician opens doors to sacred spaces and provides access to sacred wisdom of the eternal now. The listener absorbs the consciousness of the musician. Music that is created in the spirit world and brought through the spiritual musician manifests to create powerful medicine for the listener. Music that is created this way can help the listener engage the imagination in powerful and meaningful ways. This kind of inspired and sacred music infuses the imagination with the awareness of expanded perception and allows the listener to perceive beyond what is normally possible. The listener can more easily receive messages from his inner being and other beings in alternate dimensions.

The spiritual musician has a responsibility to the highest spiritual Masters to relinquish any desires and completely let go of any identity that he may have carried. The spiritual musician is no longer considered to be an individual; he is a part of the universal cosmic message that music carries. He is a messenger of the cosmic message of unconditional and unlimited love. The spiritual musician has died into the music and is born into the message. An example of this is the ancient musicians of India who must first be experienced yogis, spiritually advanced people who provide the listener with access to sacred wisdom through sacred vibration—music.

CHAPTER THREE

Music and the Spirit

◻   ◻   ◻

Music as a Reflection
of the Collective Consciousness

Ancient music rests deeply in the spiritual ideals, and ancient temple music was played to maintain balance in humans, flora, fauna, Mother Earth, the solar system, the galaxy and the universe. The purpose of ancient temple music was to keep the cosmic connection in place and in balance. It is commonly thought that audible sound is a bridge to beyond the physical world. Music is a reflection of activity in other dimensions and is used to keep in tune with the necessary evolutionary changes in cosmic sound. The universe is continually transforming, and we must shift our vibrational frequency to stay parallel with the transformations.

Every life form on Mother Earth resonates at a particular frequency, and the sum of these frequencies corresponds to the frequency of Mother Earth. Mother Earth offers us a vibrational reflection of the solar system, which reflects the frequencies of the Universe. These frequencies, from the universe to the individual human, animal and plant, correspond to particular musical notes. Music offers us the possibility and provides us the tools for tending to our responsibility of being pro-active in maintaining our cosmic connection.

Humans have been creating music since the beginning of our existence on Earth. All civilizations have created musical instruments and have played music within the context of ceremony, ritual, and prayer. Many ancient cultures played music to honor and communicate with the gods and deities they looked to for guidance. The Egyptians and Greeks, the Bamana, Soso, Malinke, and Wolof of West Africa, the Ethiopians, Baganda, Acholi, and Kikuyu of East Africa, the Mayan, Zapotec, Mixtec and Aztec of Central and South America—most ancient cultures have creation stories filled with the power of sound and music and have created music for specific spiritual purposes. These are just a few examples of the many indigenous cultures that use music in this way.

In addition, indigenous cultures have a long history of looking beyond the physical world for social and spiritual guidance, and many recognize music and the drum as powerful spiritual tools to awaken and heal our spiritual, mental and physical bodies. Many ancient cultures recognize music as universal cosmic knowledge and consider the cosmos to be the gateway to the immortal.

How is it that ancient peoples were able to know about star systems that modern science has yet to discover? The idea of an ancient technology is well-known, but there is much speculation on just what that technology is and how it is used. To access ancient information, we must travel through time to the place where knowledge resides. This is the same place where the ancients were able to access it, and we can use the same methods that were used thousands of years ago. The method is music. Music does not know space, and it lives in time. Universal time is not linear but circular, so past, present and future exist in the here and now. Universal time is accessible with music. Music is a prayer, and sacred energies are released when music is played and songs are sung.

The music we create is a reflection of our collective consciousness. Our music tells our story, speaking of our priorities, ideals and morals, and it embodies our beliefs and thoughts. Our music either forms the invisible boundaries of our self-made prison or reveals to us a path to the divine, the endless and infinite.

Nature holds a key to universal sounds that we have considered to be and defined as music. The sounds of nature call to a deep and primal place within our being. They connect us to Mother Earth and, ultimately, the universe. The sounds of nature offer us divine inspiration to create music that bridges the outer world, the seen worlds, the inner world, the unseen and the spiritual worlds. Music inspired by nature can be found in every region of Mother Earth and every period of time. The songs of the birds inspire flight, the songs of crickets inspire deep reflection, the songs of the frogs inspire us to keep walking an inner path, and the songs of the wolves and coyotes connect us to the stars. The natural world is filled with music, and music fills the natural world. Our humanness and our ability to bridge the seen and unseen allow us to connect with the music of the natural world to create a balance for all living beings.

Music is the Fabric of Community
within the Bamana Society

Let's look at an indigenous culture to illustrate how we have used music to bridge the physical and spiritual worlds and to rebalance, inspire and bring harmony to all living beings. Many indigenous social structures are predicated on spiritual belief systems, and many indigenous societies have had such social systems in place for thousands of years and have produced spiritually advanced peoples with communicative abilities reaching beyond the physical realm. Such abilities give humans the opportunity to access the invisible realm to affect the physical world.

Africa offers a perspective on spirituality that illustrates the value of connection to the invisible and the ability of humans to manipulate energy. Her connection to nature, her community and her creativity in expression are all aspects of human spirituality many have forgotten. For the Bamana people of modern-day Mali, West Africa, these practices are an integral part of life. The connection to the spirit realms is a necessary element in the social structure and is used to maintain the physical, mental, emotional, and spiritual health of the community. The Bamana perspective on spirituality is based on taking action in the physical world to access energy in the invisible world and using it to manifest change back in the physical world. The community has a foundation in personal and community relationships to the invisible world, meaning the community that collectively engages the invisible world is physically, emotionally, mentally, and spiritually healthy. This is achieved in everyday interactions with community members in secular and sacred spaces. In pre-colonial times, there was no space dedicated to worship, as worship is living every day and in every place.

For the Bamana and most indigenous cultures, music is the fabric of the culture. It is the thread that binds the individual to the community and the community to the spirit realm. In every circumstance, music is used to create connection and meaning and strengthen purpose. Music is a language of the spirit, and the act of playing music creates a bridge from the physical to the spiritual. Music provides us a direct connection to the spirit realm and allows for community members to focus their energy and intentions toward any given goal or task. Therefore the health of the community is also reflected in the music it plays. The music of the Bamana reflects a sincere contentment and a joy in being alive. The Bamana weave rhythms together like water flowing briskly down a freshwater stream. The individuals are connected on unspoken levels and maintain a strong connection no matter what. It is as if their molecules are dancing together, so that when one shifts position musically, the others adjust without missing a beat.

In village life, music is a part of everything, and the drum is the primary instrument. The music's role is dependent on the occasion, and every song has an intention and a purpose. The occasions are as diverse as healings, rituals, farming and harvesting, fishing, gathering, hunting, journeys and celebrations such as full moons, weddings, baptisms, funerals and naming ceremonies. Songs are played for occupations such as warrior, teacher, farmer, fisher, hunter and sorcerer. Sometimes age groups receive the honor of a particular rhythm. Elders certainly play a vital role in society, so there are numerous rhythms for them. Children and women also receive a selection of rhythms, honoring them for their contributions to the society. Whenever music is played, the women sing songs of protection. This is a vital part of any celebration or ceremony where music is present. Every time music is played, the village is vulnerable. Doorways to the spirit realms are opened, and measures are taken to ensure the safety of the villagers.

The Bamana society prioritizes an interconnection among community members, the earth and the spirit realms. Within a society that places emphasis on interconnection, there is a social structure that provides a foundation for the proliferation of this interdependence. To understand how the Bamana have been successful in creating a culture that supports this, we need to look at how the society is designed. The Bamana operate under a social structure laced with tradition. Tradition serves to maintain a fluid social order through the generations and preserves the ideology of the culture. It is important that when we think of tradition or traditional ways that we recognize them to be dynamic concepts rather than static identities. A tradition has a foundation in the ways of our forefathers but also maintains a space for innovation and evolution. While it may be that the social structure, in terms of specific categories of people, has changed, the foundation contained in the ideology of social relationships has not. Therefore, in the village, the Bamana have maintained a social space in which relationship and proximity to the invisible are important ideologies, and music is the key to the door of multidimensional time and space.

In pre-colonial times, the Bamana, like many other African indigenous societies, functioned socially within a tripartite social system that consisted of farmers (nobles), specialized workers, and slaves. The concept of the noble probably began with the foundation of the Mali Empire in the thirteenth century. It is probable that the notion of the slave and specialized worker existed before the development of the Mali Empire. Eventually, slavery was outlawed and the traditional society functioned with the help of the farmer and specialized worker.

For the Bamana, the specialized workers, called Nyamakala, provide the necessary tools for sustained living and offer the society services regarding the invisible realm as well. Nyamakala can be broken down to nyama—"life energy"—and kala—"handle." So the Nyamakala are the handles of power or points of access to the life-giving energy of the universe. The Bamana's willingness to authenticate and honor the invisible realms by recognizing their existence and their participation in it strengthens a collective belief that we are a part of the universe and that we are connected to energy outside our physical proximity. The Bamana's social structure lends itself to supporting these community beliefs and therefore strengthening individual and communal bonds to the invisible.

The Nyamakala comprise the following clans: the Jeli, the musicians and oral transmitters of history; the Garanke, the leather workers; the Kassa, the farmers; and the Numu, the blacksmiths. These clans are endowed with the rights to spiritual and technological skills that enable them to offer specialized services to the society. The musicians, or Jeli, hold a special role in traditional West African culture. The responsibility of playing music is no small affair. The music itself may heal an illness, cure a disease or, on the other hand, kill a person. The intent of the musician plays an important part of the outcome in a ceremonial situation. The Jeli belong to a lineage of Jeli, so one is born into that role and he is responsible for passing down the culture's history and knowledge to the next generations, therefore he is held in high esteem and respected throughout the land. The Jeli must be disciplined both physically and mentally. He must be able to endure hours of playing music and protect the village from unseen forces such as unwanted spirits and entities. He must be committed, humble, passionate and balanced within himself to uphold his duties.

Often, the connection to the invisible comes to fruition through intermediaries such as nature. Therefore, the Bamana's spiritual experience is manifested through the social structure, which inherently connects people to people and people to nature. Music is the social fabric of the Bamana and it defines spirituality within the social constructs of the culture. The Bamana social system is organized in such a way that they do not have designated priests who have abilities to access the spiritual realm. Rather, certain clans have access to certain areas of the spiritual worlds. Beyond this, people belonging to specific Nyamakala within the clan each have specific abilities concerning different areas of the spiritual. For instance, the blacksmith (Numu) is widely recognized for his abilities in dealing with the invisible. Through the forging process, he comes into contact with the most powerful energies. It is said that the forging of iron is the place where life meets death and is again reborn. It is for this reason that the smith is often regarded as being the most capable of carrying out certain spiritual practices. The Numu will often request that music be played when he is forging iron. The musicians will come to play specific rhythms and songs for the Numu. The music allows the Numu to communicate more efficiently with the spiritual realms, where the energy for the forging comes from. It is said that the design and form of the djembe, a popular Bamana drum, was created at the request of the Numu.

Public and private life are connected in such a way that

the person engages the community on emotional and personal levels that require a personal vulnerability that produces an environment of openness among community members. For example, children are accountable to all adults in the village and all adults are responsible for all children. In the West, we often hesitate to discipline others' children. In Bamana culture, we would be obliged to do so. This kind of social structure leaves no room for secrets and produces an environment of personal integrity and responsibility that aid in the development of the consciousness. The Bamana call this personal integrity "dambe". "Dambe "is a very old term that implies that a person has "integrity in the light of God". It is bestowed on someone who has shown tremendous wisdom, kindness, compassion and humility over a period of time. Having "dambe" is important because it is in who you are and what others know of you that defines your role in the community. This concept exceeds life in this body and affects the soul's position in society in the next life as well. The belief in reincarnation is commonplace within the Bamana, and oftentimes it is known, through ritual and communication with the invisible, who is being reborn. The reputation of the person in the physical world is a reflection of the soul position in the invisible realm and therefore has great importance regarding the newborn.

The Bamana practice ancestry worship, which exemplifies their connection to the invisible. Ancestral worship is pervasive and dictates moral behavior among the people. For the Bamana, death is a transition from the physical to the invisible and is not the end of the soul's experience, only a change in status. It is an intermediary step from the physical to the spirit world. The Bamana consider the invisible realm to be an integral part of life, and ancestry worship is a vital aspect of Bamana social life that connects the person to the invisible.

The concept of death and rebirth is reflected in the Bamana's work in agriculture. For the Bamana, agriculture is not only the means of providing food for the society but a vital aspect of their spiritual ideology; for the soul, under the appropriate circumstances, will be reborn and live again in human form. This idea is similar to the seed that "dies" when buried in the earth only to be "reborn" in an endless variety of forms. Therefore, when the farmer plants his seeds, he is not only providing food for the community but continuing the unending circle of life and death.

The connection to nature is developed initially through activities such as agriculture and initiation. Respect for the land is obvious when we learn of our dependence on it. It is understood that destroying the land is ultimately destroying oneself. Children are born into the Nyamakala of their fathers, including the Kassa, the Numu, the Garanke and the Jeli. Each Nyamakala produces new members by way of initiation, which always involves a sometimes-lengthy introduction to nature. Often the young bilakoro, or uninitiated boys, will be required to spend a significant amount of time in nature. They are to use this time to learn the secrets of nature and gain the knowledge required to survive.

The Bamana believe the world is full of different types of entities that offer different types of knowledge to man and that it is up to man to discover them. This knowledge, called Jiridon, is the knowledge of nature, or the "science of the trees." Use of this knowledge requires the use of various combinations of plants, vegetables and certain inorganic matter. No single man has knowledge of all Jiridon; rather, certain clans specialize in certain Jiridon.

The knowledge of energy is important in the Bamana society. Energy is everywhere around us; all material in the physical world as well as everything unseen are made of energy. For the Bamana, the acquisition of knowledge regarding energy is fundamental for the growth of humanity. Once knowledge is obtained, it must be organized into configurations that allow people to use it. These configurations are called "daliluw." Daliluw (dalilu, sing.) are compact, concise units of knowledge containing large amounts of concentrated energy and information used for the completion of particular activities. Daliluw are designed to collect this energy en masse and are empowered by traditional knowledge in the form of information. Daliluw provide the power contained within human acts. Many daliluw can be activated only with the aid of a kind of secret speech called "kilisi." Kilisi consists of the whispering and chanting of certain phrases while the daliluw is being prepared. Furthermore, the daliluw are infused with a small amount of the preparers' saliva. Speech and saliva are full of nyama. Different clans own certain kinds of daliluw for particular purposes and thus provide specialized services regarding the invisible.

The passing of information and knowledge through the generations is vital to the society on many levels. With the absence of an official written word, the society depends on the oral transmission of knowledge for survival. Bamana social arrangements dictate an oral learning process in which the individual fully participates, using all the senses in the learning experience. This kind of education through social exchange strengthens the individual's connection to the community and the invisible.

Historically, the Euro-American religious traditions place a high priority on a designated place of worship, and thus countless churches, mosques and other places of worship have been built. Pre-colonial Africa placed less importance on places of worship than their colonizers did. In fact, before colonization, buildings and structures made specifically for worship were not built in West Africa. This illustrates the fact that African Spirituality crosses into all aspects of private and public life.

Constructing buildings for the purpose of worship removes the individual from the place that harbors Spirituality, nature. In the village, people live in close proximity to the universe; they live in harmony with it and do not willingly or artificially separate themselves from it at any time. The African is in constant communication with nature, seeking harmony with the divine; therefore, it is in nature that he will establish a place of worship. The more a society departs from the traditional forms of social organization (lineage, clans and castes) in favor of the formation of a state (governmental) structure, the more importance places of worship take on. For at that point there is no longer sacred space in nature and one must be created separate from nature so that it may be maintained as sacred. We now see this in many indigenous societies, including the Bamana, because it has become commonplace for each village to have a mosque or church.

The Bamana, like so many indigenous cultures, use music in very deep and meaningful ways. Music is at the core of their relationships with each other, Mother Earth, their ancestors and the spirit realms. They have developed and refined this technology to such a degree that music has become a medicine that is used daily, in whatever context is currently occurring. Music is the application of intention originating in the physical and sent to the spiritual to be rearranged and sent back to the physical. The Bamana, like many others, are masters of the language of music. They recognize music's ability to hold energy and, like daliluw, can manipulate it to manifest positive change and transformation for all beings.

This spiritual technology is available to all of us. We can look to the cultures of the past and those still with us that use music as a powerful spiritual tool for inspiration and guidance. Everything they have learned and developed is available to us. The secret is music and the drum. Accessing ancient spiritual technology is possible when we know how to use music to access the book of time. Then we are able to read any page at any time. Again, it is music that offers us the possibility of accessing this knowledge and transforming our lives forever.

CHAPTER FOUR

The Practice of Becoming

□   □   □

Who Am I?

We are born in a specific place and time, with roles, rules and regulations we are asked to follow. This "training" forms the foundations of our personality, beliefs, thoughts and actions. The process of becoming has always been heavily influenced by the culture of the society that surrounds us. If we look around the globe at different cultures, we will see that each one has created a unique but often-similar perception of what it means to be human and what the process of becoming offers us. This criterion sets the stage for our training to be productive members of society. We will develop focused ways of thinking, being and behaving within the society, and we will begin a journey of becoming who we are trained to become.

Many ancient cultures hold the perception that humans conspire with the gods to co-create their world in a way that supports a connection with unseen worlds. Many of these cultures believe that the most efficient method of creating change and transformation in the physical world is to access the invisible, the realm of creation, destruction, constant change, and the spirit worlds. They believe we arrived here on Earth from these worlds, and we must not forget to maintain a strong connection to our origins as cosmic walkers and universal souls—those who travel the universe in service of the light that creates, destroys and transforms all things, visible and invisible. They are the ones who allow our hearts to beat collectively. They are intuition. They are the fleeting moments of connectedness we feel when we sing, dance and play music. Cosmic walkers are inside all of us and we are all universal souls, taking the time on earth to breathe, love and practice alchemy in a magical world of unlimited possibilities.

For we who reside in the 21st century among the modern comforts that modernity provides us, it is easy to forget who we are, where we have come from, where we are going and how we are going to get there. As modern technology evolved, humanity began to slowly forget that we could fly with the gods and that we can conspire with them to create a life on Earth that supports the Universal life energy we are all created from. Granted, modernity has provided us with technology that can save lives, provides a kind of connectedness via the Web and other communication systems and offers pleasantries and comforts that many of us enjoy. But this has come at a price, the loss of our cosmic memory.

Today, many are beginning to awaken and remember who we are, where we come from, and where we are going. We are beginning a new kind of training that enables us to expand our awareness, transform our perception and open to the magic of life. We are human beings connected to the invisible, the unseen, and the many worlds of Spirit. The cosmic memory of our journey comes when we are ready to let go of the linear training, turn our thoughts upside down and stop asking "why" and begin asking "when" and "how." When we lose the desire to understand before taking action and redefine words like trust, compassion, and love, when we are ready to learn to see, hear and feel in a new way—one that does not utilize the five senses, but uses the higher knowing that resides inside our being—then our cosmic memories, dormant for many ages and waiting for us to remember and engage, return to us.

The Power of the Drum

Now is the time. We have access to one of the most powerful tools known to humans. This tool has been waiting for us for thousands of years. Cultures around the world have used it for remembering that we are connected to each other and the universe. It is a tool that is available to all humans, young, old, big and small. The drum produces a sound that reverberates throughout our body, our being and the universe. The sound transports our spirit to the world of the ancients and connects us to the origins of the human race.

The drum has been used as a connection to our cosmic memory and a powerful tool to connect with the spirit worlds. When we play the drum, we create, strengthen and maintain this connection. We remember who we are, and we offer ourselves the opportunity to conspire with the Great Spirit to be a servant to humanity, the Earth and spirits. The drum provides us a path of becoming. Yes, you can use the drum as a tool for your own awakening. It is a simple path, but never underestimate the power of simplicity, how such a simple instrument made from nature can be a very powerful instrument of transformation in the lives of humans and how playing the drum in a sacred context can empower you to rediscover the Master Within.

Remembering Contentment

Empty the mind.
Enter knowing
and the silence
of the spirit world.
Allow judgment to dissolve.
Engage pure detachment,
allowing all to be as it is,
now, in this moment.
Float in the pools of nothingness,
the space that the mind considers
nonexistence, death
and total surrender.

There is a proverb that says, "The road to hell is paved with good intentions." How many times have we created situations where we caused pain or harm to others with our good intentions? This is because good intentions often embody our own agendas and self-centered motivations. The ego is tricky and will easily attach its own motivation to our good intentions. Pure intention embodies wisdom that allows us to escape our ego. When we release our own agenda, we can come to a place of unconditional love and pure intention. We no longer are attached to what we think we need or want, and we can more easily give of ourselves and serve others in a pure way. We can cultivate a deep sense of knowing (wisdom), compassion and humility to act on pure intentions.

The practice of becoming is really the practice of refining your intentions and remembering how to be happy. I say remembering because there is no learning; we already have everything we need inside us. It is simply a surrendering to our cosmic memory of who we are—complete, pure and one. So, how to remember happiness? What do we need to do to connect with happiness? Happiness exists separate from us and it does not need us to exist. We easily forget that it is we who have opportunities to participate in such beautiful things such as love, peace and happiness; they do not need us, rather it is we who need them. The same is true for negative energies like anger, jealousy and envy; we choose to adopt them, sometimes so quickly that we befriend anger, form a partnership with jealousy and use envy to forge a plan.

We choose to be happy. Why? Because our own inner peace and contentment are the foundation for how we navigate life. We have so many goals and aspirations, but how to reach them if we are not happy in the process and how to be when we finally reach them? It makes no sense to finally reach our goals and then not know how to be happy. Happiness is independent of our goals; it is something we must choose and practice daily. This is how emotional intelligence is developed. We are all evolving—don't miss the boat. But if you do, no worries—another one will be coming shortly.

▣   ▣   ▣

The Wisdom of the Past

Life is a revolving door of spiritual opportunities, and the past offers us opportunities for reflection. We are able to reflect on how we behaved and whether we should do anything differently in the present. In this way the past is a powerful tool for transformation. If we can learn from the past without bringing it into the present, we have used the opportunity the past offers us.

Bringing the past into the present produces more of the same experiences. When we bring the past into the present, we do not allow ourselves the opportunity for new experiences. It is like reliving a scene from a movie over and over. Many victims continue being a victim, and many who were abused now abuse others. When we bring the past into the present, we can be very predict-able. We experience the same emotions in different situations. We give the same messages and do not allow ourselves to transform. Everything in the universe changes. Change is the only certain thing in life. All beings are in a constant state of change, but so often we try to resist change. Who are we to think that we can resist the only certain thing in the universe? Let go of the past and experience freedom from negative emotions and suffering.

We can let go of the past by cultivating a practice of being here and now. We have nowhere else to be. We are here, so why resist the present moment? Resistance to anything will bring suffering. The past may contain negative experiences and events that we have attached negative emotions to. Though the events will always remain in the past, we tend to bring the past emotions into the present. Leave them in the past; they are worthless in the present.

Have a conversation with the past. Ask the past what it has to teach you. Ask the past to inform you of life's opportunities. The past is there for you, to support you, to teach you, and to allow you to grow and transform into a new being, with new messages for the world and a new way of being. If the past reminds you of your failures, your mistakes, your shortcomings and your insecurities, forgive with a deep sense of gratitude for the opportunities to see more clearly who you are. You are unlimited love, and unlimited love is the source of all creation and that is magic! Webster's dictionary defines magic as "an extraordinary power or influence seemingly from a supernatural source." As human beings, we have a unique ability to participate in these extraordinary powers. We are supernatural. Our physical bodies reside in the natural world, whereas our spiritual bodies reside in the supernatural world.

The Magic of Life

Life is magic! We are all a part of the web of life, inter-connected and interrelated on many levels. Each of us brings a unique gift to the table of the Universe, and we all have one ability in common, the opportunity to participate in magic. So, you see, we are able to be in two "places" in the same moment. Our physical bodies must stay here on earth, doing all that we do to keep it alive, but our spiritual bodies are free to be wherever we would like them to be. We can create anything we desire in the physical world by engaging an active participation with the magic of the Universe. We all have access to this kind of magic. We are all a part of it, but many of us have not been taught how to use it. Connect to the magic!

Have a meaningful conversation with your dreams, desires and hopes. We all know how to have a conversation with another person. It is easy because that conversation takes place in the physical world. The physical world provides us very tangible things to attach thoughts, ideas and concepts to. Having a conversation with your dreams, desires and hopes may seem to be a bit more difficult because you are conditioned to believe that they exist somewhere else, like the future. The future can seem so far away from the idea of you, of who you believe you are. The future, which you deem to hold your dreams, desires and hopes, seems so far that you may never reach them. If you conform to this kind of belief, you will remain here, in the same place you are now, waiting for the future to arrive and experiencing life as a series of events that just happen to you. So, what to do to change this?

It is at this moment that we all need to recognize that we have other means of communication with other beings in the supernatural worlds. As I said before, we have multiple means of being connected. The physical world offers us tangible ways of connecting to others and nature. Our spirit offers us alternate ways of connecting with others and the cosmos. Most of us do not understand how the cosmos functions and we cannot begin to comprehend the opportunities that our participation in it allows.

Connecting to the worlds of spirit allows us the opportunity to create what we desire in the physical world. We are human beings; we are a bridge between both worlds, and we have the ability to manifest in the physical world what we create in the spirit world. It is simple: Connect to your spirit. Begin with a simple ceremony; light a candle, calm your mind with music (either play an instrument or listen to your favorite and most relaxing music) and talk—out loud—to your spirit. Plant the seeds of your dreams, desires, and hopes by having a conversation with them. Empower your spirit to create what you desire by opening your heart and filling it with unlimited love for all beings, including yourself. Cultivate a deep sense of gratitude for the opportunity to participate in the Universal magic that you are given. It is a gift and should be respected, honored and revered.

◻ ◻ ◻

Duality and Non-Dualism

In many spiritual circles and traditions, we read and hear about the idea of non-dualism, the realization that there is no separation between you and me or the person and the ego. Each religion that considers this concept has defined it a little differently, but each points to the fact that the mind is relentless at wanting to create some kind of separation between itself and what it considers to be outside itself. For many, the goal of a spiritual path is to reach a state of awareness where the mind no longer places judgment on anything outside itself and accepts everything as belonging to itself. If we want to take this deeper we could say that this state of awareness is beyond the mind altogether, a place of no mind where the mind no longer identifies with anything other than the realization of complete oneness with everything visible and invisible, physical and spiritual. For many, this state of awareness is enlightenment and is the highest state of awareness available to us.

◨   ◨   ◨

The Seen and Unseen

There is another kind of duality we experience on the path of the Spirit. Being human offers us a dual existence. Our spirit lives in the domain of the invisible, while our bodies reside in the physical. Humans have the unique experience of existing in both realms. Since the beginning of our presence on Earth as humans, we have utilized the realms of the spirit to manifest in the physical. Ancient cultures have shown us that making and maintaining our connection to the invisible is a powerful way to exist in the physical. When we participate in the realms of the spirit, we connect to a consciousness that gives meaning to the physical. Our humanness is complete when we access the spirit. We engage a set of rules beyond our current and modern understanding and beyond the laws of nature and physics. We are able to manipulate energy to create change and transformation in the physical. Many people refer to this as magic.

The seen world, material or physical, can be described as the world perceived through our senses and the world perceived through our mind (reason). Our minds provide us the function of reason, which dictates the way we interact with the world and our judgment. The unseen world can be further described as things we associate with the spirit world such as energy and intuition. The seen world, as perceived through our senses, gives the person an apparent vision of a world with known rules, laws and limitations. We have and continue to build foundations on the laws that seem to govern our existence on earth. Our senses allow us the pleasure, and sometimes displeasure, of taste, touch, smell, sound and sight, while our mind gives us the capability of reason, thus allowing us to interpret and analyze our sensory input as well as make decisions regarding the perceived reality of the world.

The unseen world exists much further beyond and deeper than the experience of seeing the world through our senses allows us to perceive. Within the material world, all known laws and properties apply, but it is often the case that our senses overwhelm and dominate our notion of the world, and it is easy for many to remain complacent living only within the material, sensible world. It is our senses that offer us access to the seen world, and it is also the senses that limit our access to only the seen world. The human experience offers us access to both worlds. If we can reach into our self and begin to see with spiritual eyes, we can access the unseen world, where reality exists as much as we allow it to. I mean that the unseen, spiritual worlds or dimensions exist beyond what our mind is capable of imagining. Each energy center of the body, or chakra, contains an eye that we can look through to see the secrets of the universe. Each chakra is a gateway or portal to other dimensions, to our origins, and to our cosmic memory that links us to a purity of source that is love. One of the keys to unlocking and opening the portal doors of our chakras is music.

Music bridges the gap between our intention and other dimensions. It enables our spirit to slip into the portal of our solar chakra and to dance into other dimensions.

The unseen world has its own rules and laws, those independent of the seen world and those that allow us to perceive the living world, consisting of both the seen and unseen worlds, differently. The seen and unseen worlds exist interdependently, meaning they co-exist in the same time, with some humans relying on both worlds for direction and guidance. Therefore, the perception of the seen world may change once we have accessed the unseen world. The vitality, power and energy contained within the region of the unseen world may give us motivation, strength and courage in both worlds. Energy is the conduit of life. Ever changing, undying and eternal, it is everything, and we are everything.

Access to the unseen world offers us tools we may use in our existence in the seen world. Patience, listening, discipline, courage and wisdom are all experiences that may be enhanced by making use of the unseen world. The seen world offers us tools to be used in gaining access to the unseen world. An activity that requires high levels of discipline may give us the patience, time, space and courage to focus enough energy in one place to open the door to the unseen world. In this way one learns that the key to transcendence (to the unseen world) is in the person co-existing in both worlds. The problem is only one of perception. Our perceptions appear to dictate the limitations of the seen world when the seen world lives within the unseen world. The unseen world penetrates the seen world and enhances our perceptions if we use the tools necessary to achieve this. When we are able to bring the awareness and wisdom from our experiences in the unseen worlds into our lives in the seen world, we carry a perception that guides our actions throughout our life. The foundation of our priorities has changed, and a deep inner knowing of the purpose of life and our mission in it has developed us into beings who are content in any situation and therefore ready and able to be good servants to our purpose. We will let any distractions live in another world and enjoy the seen world from a deep perspective of detachment because we know we live a dual existence and we know which one is a dream and which one is not.

Create Your Reality

Creating our own reality is our greatest asset in life.

This means we have the ultimate authority over how we feel, what we think and how we act. We have the final say on how far and wide we are able to see into the seen and unseen. It is this very realization that may either enhance or oppress our perception. When we are able to perceive or see above and beyond the limitations of our mind, the possibilities of our reality are eternal. Our reality comprises everything sensible and insensible. It is the insensible that may make it possible to have meaningful and purposeful experience of the many possibilities of our reality.

This idea of non-dualism is important and relevant; it is a step forward in the evolution of the spirit. It is not the end goal of the spirit. The spirit is capable of much more than occupying space in the vast universe and beyond. Our spirits do not desire to reach enlightenment for the sake of reaching enlightenment. Our spirits desire to be of service to that which it is a part of, the divine, and the sacred—unconditional love. The sincere motivation to be of service will take us to the appropriate states of awareness that we need in order to take action.

I want to share a prayer with you that reminds us to re-main in a place of humility while we participate in the magic of life and the universe.

It was not I who healed
But for the powers from the outer worlds
And the visions and ceremonies
Had made me like a hole
Through which the power could come
To the two-legged and four-legged.
If I thought it was myself doing the healing
The hole would disappear
and no power would come through it.

- Chief Black Elk, Oglala Sioux

CHAPTER FIVE

Mission and Purpose

◙   ◙   ◙

The Illusion of Freedom

How is it that so many of us live an entire life without knowing what our purpose and mission are? Our culture places value on a set of priorities that lie outside the development of community relationships and connection to others, nature and the spirit realms. Americans define themselves by and place value on individual freedoms rather than prioritize the role of the individual within a communal context. Individual rights take precedence over the needs of the community. This is significant because a culture that prioritizes interconnection between community members also develops a natural connection with the earth and the spiritual realms. Given that, the society that prioritizes a spiritual ideology that places emphasis on interconnection also develops a social structure that provides a foundation and support system for such interconnection.

Modern-day humans relinquish their connection to the spiritual for the continuance of the status-inspired Euro-American traditions. The abandonment of spiritual connection has created spiritual and emotional poverty for many people around the globe. The manifestation of spiritual and emotional poverty of this sort manifests in the social constructs of the society. This poverty offers us the illusion of freedom. It produces people who have lost the ability, or haven't realized the maturity, to critically observe the visible and invisible worlds around them. We perceive that we are free and have freedom, but we are not able to see the extent of the kind of freedoms that are available to us.

Many of us have spent our time trying to please others or fit into social groups or the workplace. We are taught to be motivated by receiving praise from others rather than developing an inner knowing of who we are. Instead of looking inside for what we need, we have been taught to look outside. You have everything you could ever want or need inside you!

The underlying question we must answer is this: Are you a human having a spiritual experience or a spiritual being having a human experience? The answer to this question will form the foundation of your beliefs and shape your thoughts and actions. Those who choose to be humans having spiritual experiences may have intermittent revelations and epiphanies, but they will ultimately spend their time in the physical world searching for the next spiritual experience to satisfy their desire to be connected and experience inner peace. Life will become a series of events that happen to them and will struggle to maintain a connection to the sacred wisdom of their inner being. Those who choose to be spiritual beings having a human experience will begin to perceive the world and all it has to offer from a spiritual perspective. Life will become an adventure, and they will find themselves following their passion, finding their mission and living life with a deep sense of inner peace.

Purposeful Living

We are all here for a purpose and have a mission to fulfill, and everyone must know his or her purpose in this life. Finding our purpose and mission should be our first priority. Everything else will be set into place when we realize what it is we are here to do. Each of us is unique and has agreed to a mission before coming into this body. How do we know what our purpose and mission is? Purpose grows from passion, so your mission will be something you are passionate about and something you enjoy so much that you could spend every day for the rest of your life doing. Find your passion and you will find your mission.

Purpose is not who you are; rather, it is a manifestation of who you are. Your purpose is monitored by spirit in the unseen world. The Great Spirit and Masters have authorized your purpose, you have agreed and volunteered and this is why you have a physical body. The purpose of a human being is to serve using the gifts provided to you from spirit. Everyone brings to this world a gift, something important that he/she must deliver in this lifetime. In the past and in many indigenous cultures, the community is obligated to help each person remember and deliver the gift. Failure to recognize your purpose places one in a constant state of crisis.

Learning Is Remembering

We are born with a memory of ourselves. This memory contains all we have been, all we are, and all we will be. This is our cosmic memory and it can help us connect to our purpose in this lifetime. We are trained to think that we need to learn everything. Our education tells us that we must learn good manners. If we remember who we are and the love we are born of, then living a life of compassion and unlimited love provides us a more-than-adequate foundation of good manners. Certain things, specific to the culture we are a part of, are good to learn. I like the idea of learning how to repair my vehicle or work with imaging software. These are good to learn, but we do not need to learn how to be ourselves. We do not need to learn how to walk a spiritual path and be connected to all things seen and unseen. We need to remember who we are and what we are made of.

Learning is remembering what you already know. The foundation of a person's ability to participate in the connectivity of all living things is formed by the knowledge and awareness of one's intuition and the skill of inner listening. These are key aspects to navigating a spiritual geography. The human spirit is the gateway to the invisible. The soul can interpret intuition and other psychic abilities that lie in the unseen world. When we relax and open our heart, we are granted the opportunity to receive messages to aid us in the process of spiritual development, or the process of manifesting your purpose in this lifetime.

The soul is similar to the eye in this context. When we learn the skill of looking through the peripheral vision of our soul, we will have access to a purity of truth that can guide us in making decisions. All people already contain all the knowledge they need, but working with a mentor to help them remember what they know is helpful. The relationship between the student and mentor must be motivated by love. Increasing clarity and maturity in the student motivates the process of mentoring. Ultimately, the relationship between mentor and mentee will be focused on finding the mentee's purpose and place in life. The process unravels the mentee's tangled web of rules, judgments, and attachments and allows the mentee to create a new reality that allows passion, creativity, and freedom.

Our purpose and mission is nonnegotiable.

As long as we stay committed to our purpose and mission, we will be taken care of. The Universe provides all that is needed to support this commitment. We must commit fully to our mission and make it our first priority in life. The universe wants you to succeed and will conspire to allow for the opportunities to manifest in your life. It is up to us to recognize them and jump into the opportunities of life.

Align your life with your mission.

Most people would rather play it safe and stay within a comfort zone that is unsatisfying than take risks, change or move towards a direction that they know will provide them what they are really looking for. The key is getting your priorities aligned with your spiritual goals, purpose and mission. To do this you must live life with passion. Without passion you will never succeed. Whatever you are involved in, you should be passionate about it. Your work and relationships will provide you only with what you provide them.

Listen to your heart.

Go within to find answers. Friends and family may have good intentions, but you are the only one who knows what is best for you. Trust your instincts, reflections and intuition and you are on your way to a more purposeful and meaningful life.

Stick to your passion, purpose and mission with unwavering devotion and the Universe will conspire to give you everything you want and need. Throw caution to the wind, be wild and dive headfirst into your new life. Be bold and brave to live your dreams!

Since I was young, I knew I wanted to play drums. I can remember being nine years old and listening to the legendary band Led Zeppelin on the concert show the local radio station played every Saturday night. In the middle of the show, within a song called Moby Dick, there was a drum solo that shook my soul. John Bonham, the drummer for the band, played with such passion, and the way he played led me to a place of enchantment. I was spellbound by the energy in his solo. Then I heard something different; the sound of the drums had changed. I realized he was no longer using his drumsticks. He had thrown away his sticks and was using his hands! My first thought was "ouch"! How could he do that, just hitting those drums with his hands? I knew the drums had metal rims that held the skins to the shells, and I knew he must have been hitting his hands against those metal rims. Within a moment I realized he didn't care. He was in a trance and completely in love with those drums and embodied by the spirits of the drum. His passion was contagious and overtook my whole being. I knew in that moment that I was going to be a drummer.

John Bonham showed me that, in his opinion, any rules that existed with music were meant to be broken. He inspired me to play music exactly the way I felt it and not to be afraid to express that feeling no matter what others thought or said.

That night shaped my destiny, and for many years playing drums is all I thought about. I was nine years old. At age 12 I got a job as a paperboy, delivering newspapers around the neighborhood. I had a long route and it became a lot of work. After school I would come home, stuff papers with extra ads or whatever had to be inserted that day and make multiple trips on my bicycle to complete the route. Around that time, I was transferred to a new school where I had the option to learn a musical instrument. I chose the snare drum, as it was the only drum available to me there. I was so happy to bring home that drum and spend many hours learning the exercises they gave me. My mother, however, was not so happy with the sound of the snare drum. At the time, I could not understand her discontent with the sound—I loved it! I was exiled to the garage, the only place in the house that did not have people in it. I don't think my mother realized how a garage could turn into an amplifier when it was empty. Soon, the neighbors were calling to complain and my snare-drum days were over.

It was maybe three or four more years before I began playing again. We had moved to another house in the same town. By then I had saved money from the paper route that I'd had for so many years. I was now 16 years old. I asked my mother and father for a meeting, and we sat as I told them I wanted to buy a drum set and begin playing. The conversation turned into the classic "What are you going to do when you grow up?" talk that parents have with their children. I said I wanted to play drums. They said something like "Yes, yes, that is a nice hobby, but what do you want for a career?" I said I wanted to play in a band, travel and see the world. I didn't want to have to work, because that made everyone look so unhappy. I said that if I had to work, I wouldn't have time to play music and I would be too tired to do anything else. Finally I said I didn't want to be old and never have played music. My parents were very patient with me and calmly said that I could play music but that I should have a backup plan in case my music dreams did not happen.

I held my breath for an eternity, it seemed. I had never thought about the possibility that it wouldn't happen. I felt the fear and anxiety that this thought brought with it. I didn't know what to say. I changed the subject back to the drum set. I told them I wanted to buy a drum set and play it in my bedroom. They looked at each other and told me the meeting was adjourned and they would call me back to the table when they were ready. I left and went to my room. It felt as if my entire future was being discussed, and I resented the fact that two other people were responsible for approving or disapproving of it. I made some phone calls to friends to ask them if I could either keep my drum set at their house or, if worse came to worse, come live there with the drum set and play it every day. I had a friend whose parents were not really around much, and I knew I could live there if I needed to. Soon, my parents called me back to the table. They told me I could get the drum set and play every day until nine o'clock in the evening, as long as my schoolwork was finished and I ate dinner at the table with the family. I was so happy.

That night I went to bed, but something was not right. I had this fear that I might not be able to do this, play music, and that it might have to be just a hobby that I pursued at night and on weekends. This feeling was sickening to me; it paralyzed me and I could not sleep. I put on some of my favorite music at the time, Pink Floyd, and fell asleep. Not far into the dream time, I awoke, but I was not in my room. I was in space, in another world. I could not see anything I recognized, and everything seemed foreign. I was floating atop a soft ball of light, and there were other balls of light all around me, but no one else was there. I felt curious and a little afraid, but somehow I knew this was a safe place. It had a strange sense of home that made we feel welcome and safe. After some time, I heard a voice. It asked me if I was afraid. I said that I was not afraid to be here but that I was afraid I could not play music and things would not work out for me if I didn't get a career or regular job. The voice said, "No matter what you think or feel, you must always know that if you stay true to your passion, you will always be taken care of. Others who love you will do their best to save you from their fears, but you must recognize that they are not your fears and you do not have to own them. Now go to sleep." I awoke the next morning lying in my bed and in my room. I was so happy to have been wherever I was the night before.

A part of me wanted to go back there. As I lay in bed, I remembered the message from the night before. It was planted so deep in my psyche that I knew I would never forget it, and I knew I would need to use it throughout my life.

The next day I began the search for a used drum set. Within a month I had started a band, and my parents' basement was our rehearsal space. I played my first gig at age 17 with my best friend and guitar player. The name of the band was Celebration Day. We had no bass player, and we thought the best way to find one was to play gigs and advertise at the show. We eventually found a bass player and all played together for a few years. I joined other bands and found myself playing music every night of the week and all day Saturday and Sunday. Some of the bands I joined were in neighboring towns, and I drove an hour each way to practice and gigs. Music became my passion, provided me with a sense of meaning and purpose and kept me out of trouble. I found that I would rather play music than do anything else. While many of my friends were out partying or getting into trouble, I was at home practicing and reinventing myself on the drums. Music saved my life;

my passion for music gave me the insight to see that I could be anything, do anything, break all the rules and live a creative life. I enjoyed the thought of walking a road less traveled and searching for my path on that road. I knew my life would be a big adventure as long as I was committed to my passion, and as long as I let nothing come between music and me, I would succeed.

One of the bands I was in recorded an album, and we decided to book a tour. We had meetings, figured out where we wanted to go and searched for club contacts. We divided the contacts between me and the bass player. We booked the tour for the following spring and found ourselves driving around the Midwest for six weeks. It was my first taste of life on the road, and I enjoyed the freedom of traveling and, strangely enough, the stress of trying to find free places to stay and not having enough money for food or gas to get to the next show. In my eyes, the tour was a success just because we completed it.

After returning to my hometown, I felt inspired by the tour experience and continued to play as much as I could. I could feel the day I would leave my hometown coming closer. I knew I had to leave to have any chance of tasting success in the music industry. My hometown had never been known to attract any record-industry leaders, and I didn't think they were going to begin looking there any time soon.

I began playing with another band located about an hour's drive from my city. My life was filled with music, but I was also in a relationship with a young woman who had a child. Her boy was not my child, but regardless, I enjoyed being with them both. I enjoyed being "daddy" in the evenings and on weekends, and I enjoyed the fact that we did not live together. We both lived with our parents. She was in school and I was already married to my music. I knew one day I would have to make a decision about this. I knew she was searching for a father figure for her son, someone to be there consistently and long term. One day she approached me and said she wanted me to be a father to her son; she suggested we get married. I was happy and honored. I loved her and her child, and I knew that one day I would want this, but that day was not now. I had other things I had to do before I got married and had children. I asked her for 24 hours to reflect.

I was employed by my father at that time as a graphic and layout designer for a small publication company he owned. The job was good, and it gave me a good opportunity to spend more time with my father. Life was moving along. I enjoyed the work the job offered me and the business lunches with my father and his clients. My nights and weekends were filled with playing music and spending time with my girlfriend and her child. I found myself beginning to create a fantasy bubble where life was moving along with a strange sense of stability that I could, even more strangely, imagine myself sinking into. When I considered the notion of sinking deeper into the life that was taking shape, it made me uncomfortable, to say the least. I knew I would leave one day and thought that day might come sooner rather than later.

The day after my girlfriend proposed marriage, I was at work trying to stay focused to make a deadline for the printer. I often worked my own hours, late into the night and sometimes overnight. That was one of the perks of the job; I could work whenever I wanted as long as the deadlines were met. That week, however, I was at the office during regular day hours, which I sometimes did to spend time with my father. I remember being a little stressed with the deadline and having marriage on my mind. Somewhere around 2 p.m., my father called me into his office. He looked serious and excited at the same time. He wasted no time in explaining to me his plan to expand the company into new markets and how wonderful it would be if I learned how to manage and run this market while he was out expanding the business into a publishing empire.

I was stunned initially and then honored that he would consider me to run the company. I listened to the enthusiasm in his voice, and it made me happy that he thought we could be a good team. As the conversation continued, I began to have a deep realization. I looked into the future and saw a life that was not mine. I saw a life that had been constructed for me to show me that it was time to make the decision; it was time to jump with no parachute. Yes, I had made decisions that led me to the awful place where I was, and yes, I had considered the possibilities of this life that was now laid out in front of me, but no, I could not and would not take it. I couldn't possibly live this life and be happy, with no regrets and without looking back and wondering "what if?" I told my father that I needed to think about all this and that I did not want to make a decision without some reflection. I asked for 24 hours to reflect.

That day I left the office with the opportunity for a ready-made family and a career in place. I would probably never have to concern myself with securing a job, which I would need to support a wife and child. This was more than a job; it was a career, with stable income that was sure to grow over time. I arrived home and went to my room to think. I could feel the push to action inside my being. I thought about my girlfriend's proposal and the career opportunity. Every time I tried to make it work in my head, it just fell apart. There was no way I could ever attempt to follow my passion for music if I accepted either of these opportunities. I knew music would become a hobby and eventually die a death that only I would ever know or feel. I would be alone with this loss forever, and no one would ever understand the pain it caused me or the regret I would feel for not following my passion, my dreams, and my purpose in this lifetime.

The next day, I went into my father's office, sat down, and took a deep breath. I told him that I was very happy he wanted me to be his partner in the business and that I appreciated his trust and the friendship we had developed. I told him that I could not accept his offer, because I had to follow my dreams of playing music, and that if I did not I would spend my life regretting that I did not try. No matter how good any career opportunity looked, I could not accept it right now. I added that I needed to begin my life with music in a more serious way and that I was planning to move to a bigger city. I gave him 30 days' notice. I was going to where the music scene was booming. That city was Seattle and the year was 1991.

I called my girlfriend that afternoon. We had a sincere conversation about her proposal. It was a difficult one, but she knew what I was going to say. She knew I would leave town to follow my passion, and she knew I would be happy doing that and have regrets if I did not. We agreed that I would never come back into her child's life again after that conversation. We never spoke again.

The next couple of weeks were spent taking care of loose ends, selling my possessions, looking for a reliable vehicle and saying goodbye to friends and family. My friends had a big going-away party for me. It was surreal. I couldn't imagine that I was leaving the next day; it was something I had never done and I just could not see myself in that car, driving away . . . forever. That day came, and I surrendered to a kind of tears I had never cried as I drove on the neighborhood streets for the last time. It hit me hard, this feeling of being alone with my passion. I observed myself being so afraid of the unknown. It felt as if I had jumped into something so deep that I would never hit the ground. I had the feeling of falling into nothingness until I realized that I was not at the mercy of this feeling and that I could take action whenever I was ready. After driving on the last city street, I reached the interstate, and that is when the transformation began. As I drove out of town, I saw myself in two worlds at the same time. I was firmly placed in my vehicle driving toward my destiny. I was also very firmly placed inside my inner being and getting used to this sensation of falling until, in one moment, I began to fly. I was no longer falling uncontrollably; I had jumped with no parachute. I was willing to die, to fail and to put everything on the line and go for it. I was willing to feel the fear that arose in my being, and in the middle of it all and at the time when I needed to know how to navigate this action of jumping into my destiny, I became aware of a deeper perception that resides inside my being. I became aware of how to transform negative emotions, or in this case fear, into a deep motivation to keep going, to continue to jump again and again and again. I learned something truly valuable on that trip. I learned how to become an alchemist. I learned how to transform fear into motivation, determination, devotion and love.

I had never been to Seattle. I did not know anyone there and I did not know how I was going to make this work. I arrived seven days later, found a job and moved into my first apartment. Three days later, I was playing a drum in one of the parks located close to where I lived. I remember that I gave some attention to the desire to disappear while I was playing. I wanted to be invisible to others who were also in the park that day. Although that desire came from the thought that I did not want other people to hear me, see me or talk to me, it laid the foundation for what transpired over the next 30 minutes. The desire to be invisible and to disappear, combined with the action of drumming, created a potent cocktail that my inner being used to create a portal to another dimension.

As I played that day, I disappeared. I let go of the notion of other people. I let go of the notion that I was a person. I dissolved my identity as a human being, and I melted with the drum. I played to become the music that I heard. I played to expand my being into light. I was overwhelmed with contentment and a deep sense of peace. I looked around at the green grass and the majestic trees that surrounded me. I thought about how I wanted to find other people to play drums with. I thought about how my friends and I had started a drumming circle years ago and how I wanted to play more, learn more and go deeper with hand drumming. I believed there was so much there for me, so much that I could not see. I felt like a child, so free, and I wanted to explore. I looked up again and continued gazing at the trees. In the distance I noticed something that looked out-of-place and inconsistent with the feel of my normal perceptions. I saw a man walking around a tree and playing a drum. Immediately, I got up and began walking toward him. This was not like me, someone who wanted to disappear and become invisible to everyone. As I found myself walking toward him, I asked myself what I was doing. The answer was simple. I was going to ask him if he knew anyone who played hand drums who could teach me how to play better. This seemed a bit random to my mind at the time. Thankfully, I did not have time to question it, and before I knew it, I was standing in front of him asking him if he knew anyone who played hand drums who could teach me how to play better.

The man looked at me with a soft smile. He was dressed in a beautiful white robe with a white belt and wore no shoes. He had medium-length dark brown hair, a full beard and mustache and some hair on his forearms. He had calm, peaceful blue eyes and a soft presence. He continued walking around the tree. I could hear his thoughts. He did not actually speak out loud, but I could hear exactly what he was saying in his mind. He was asking the tree for permission to access its wisdom. He was requesting access to the knowledge of the trees, and somehow the answer to my question would come. I watched as he walked around the tree and played his drum. After the second time around the tree, I heard the tree communicate the answer back to him. I knew what he was going to tell me. As he looked at me, he spoke. He told me the name of a man, Ed, and his phone number. I thanked him and turned away to walk back to my drum. As I walked, I turned around to ascertain whether he was real or not. Of course, he was not there. The tree was there, but the man was gone. I had the name and number in my head as I picked up my things and hurried back to my apartment.

I entered and quickly put down the drum and my backpack. I picked up the phone and called the number. A man answered, and I anxiously asked for Ed. He said there was no Ed there and asked how he could help me. I told him why I was calling, and he laughed. He said that he did have a percussion group and that, although Ed was in his group, he did not live there. I smiled and said I was interested in learning more about hand drumming and asked him what kind of music the group played. He said West African percussion and asked me what I was doing that Friday night. Thinking they probably had a rehearsal scheduled, I said I was free, but as it turned out, he invited me to take part in a performance. I resisted and said that I wasn't ready for that but that I would come and watch. He asked if I could play a bell. "Well, of course I could do that," I thought. "How hard could that be?" I agreed to come and play a supporting bell part.

I got off the phone and was very excited at the possibility of a group to play with. I was not totally aware of how it happened; it all seemed like a dream. Me playing in the park, the man drumming and talking to the tree, speaking to the man, hearing his thoughts and getting the message from the tree. Finally, Friday came around and I went to the event at the location the man had specified. When I walked in, he asked if I was Martin. I responded affirmatively and he introduced himself to me. He explained that he had organized this event, where different percussion groups would come and play 30- to 45-minute sets; his group would play short sets in between so that there was no silent time. The group would also fill in if anyone canceled. The event was called "Let's Dance" and we were the Let's Dance House Band. That night, my first night, there was a cancellation and the group played for over an hour and a half. The group included my new teacher, CN, and me. He played djembe and I played bell. I loved every minute of it. I held a steady and complex bell pattern known as clave variation, and he played djembe in and around the pattern. It was like flying in a spaceship that kept changing positions. The bell pattern represented something steady, something non-changing. The djembe was showing me how to perceive the bell pattern in an infinite number of ways just by changing its phrase and intonation.

That night was the beginning of my new life. CN became my teacher, but not only of the drum. We had a unique relationship. He was older than I, was well respected and had an established position in the drumming community. CN taught me that if I wanted to learn more, I should not hesitate to let go of my ego. He taught me that having something to protect was a liability if I wanted to be on a path to self-discovery. Nothing was ever directly talked about; he never sat me down and had direct conversation with me about these things. He taught me through his actions. He was always firm and yet kind, sometimes curt, but respectful.

For the next six years I continued to study, play and perform. I began taking classes from teachers from West Africa who came through town and soon started a few other groups with friends. I was also playing drum set in bands and often rehearsed five nights a week and played gigs on weekends. My life was filled with music, and it seemed that I would someday reach my goal of making it in the music business.

I played the drum set in numerous bands and had some success with a couple of independent record labels. I managed every band I was in and learned a lot about booking gigs, CD distribution, and getting interviews and radio airplay. The last band I was in received the most success, and I knew I was on the edge of making it to my goal. I just wanted to be able to play music, pay the bills and travel, and I thought this was the way to accomplish that. Everything came to a breaking point one night. We were involved in a battle-of-the-bands contest. It was the semifinals and we were one of two bands from Seattle left in the competition. I knew we would win but was not prepared for what took place before the performance.

The band I was in was a trio featuring an acoustic stand up bass, acoustic guitar, and my very eclectic drum set, which included a kick drum, a snare drum, a floor tom, doumbeks and bongos that I played with sticks, a set of African bells, a djembe and a set of tabla I played on a few songs. The music was a mix of folk and pop. Both the guitarist and the bassist were excellent songwriters and had very different styles. Half the songs were very upbeat and danceable, and the other half were ballads; the lyrics were mostly about insecurities and sick and broken relationships. They were somehow inserted into catchy music phrases and hooks so that the audience would dance in joy most of the night. We all did our fair share of mind-altering substances, but I had vowed that I would never play a rehearsal or gig while intoxicated. I realized very young that music was my drug of choice and that consuming another drug while playing was not beneficial to me. Unfortunately, the other musicians I played with did not place the same boundaries around substances.

Before a gig one night, we were standing outside the back door. Both the guitarist and the bassist were drunk. This was not something new; they were drunk before many performances. Somehow they both managed to play great shows when they were intoxicated; it was as if the alcohol allowed them to come into a part of themselves that experienced freedom from any insecurities or fears that plagued them in their daily lives. Maybe it was the alcohol that allowed them to be on stage. Regardless, it did nothing for their ability to respect others. They were usually rude and obnoxious before the show. I stayed away until it was time to play. That night, however, I was talking with them. I said something the bassist did not like, and he struck me. I was shocked and angry. Thankfully, there was no time for me to react, as it was time for us to take the stage. I played the show angry that night. It was the first time I was not happy when playing music, and I wanted nothing more than to leave the stage. I no longer cared about the contest or the quality of the performance. I just could not see playing while I was so angry. As I continued the performance, I began to calm down and sink into the music more. I allowed the music to wash away my negative emotions, and I began to listen like I had never listened before. What came next was a message that changed my life forever.

As I played, I began to realize that the people I had in my life and the relationships I was developing were more important than anything else. I kept thinking that no one could pay me enough money to be in these sick relationships any longer. At that moment, I realized that I needed to break with the band, the industry, and my goal. I needed to make some adjustments to my goal. It was no longer enough to be successful in the music industry. I had been diligent in rewriting record contracts so that the bands I was in could retain music rights, get better royalties and generally retain more integrity. My mantra was "Do not sell out. Wait for the right deal." That night my mantra took on a deeper meaning. I realized that if I were to continue with this group of people, I would be selling out my best interests: this newly found goal of being healthy and around healthy people. I hesitated and thought that if I continued for a while and we won the competition, maybe something would come from it and I would have choices about whom I played with. By the end of the performance, I was solid in my decision. I was going to quit the group. I was done with the substance abuse and emotional drama of the group and most of the groups I had been in.

After the show, a man came up to me and asked who the manager was. I said I was and asked how I could help him. He looked at me, handed me a packet of papers, and said that I should look it over and that we would meet at 9 a.m. the next morning to complete the deal. He gave me his card and said to call him tonight to arrange for the location. I took the package and knew what it was. I said nothing to the others, packed up my drums and went home. Upon returning to my apartment, I sat down and opened the package. It was from a very popular record company and was for more money than I thought I would ever see in my lifetime. After reading it, I knew that I would have to change some things before I agreed to sign it, but I also knew in that moment that it would never happen. I had made my decision and was not going to sign something I believed would place me in a long-term situation of having to deal with the drama and dysfunction of the group. I knew things would only get worse if we actually had success. I had seen it many times before. The band feels solid and together until success comes, and that is the beginning of the end for many ensembles.

The feeling I had in that moment was not one I would have expected. If I had thought about it, I would have expected to feel anxiety and fear. I had no alternate plan for my life; I had put all my energy into this path and had no idea what was next for me. Instead, I felt a deep sense of freedom and the sensation of euphoria. I was almost ecstatic at the notion that I had completed this part of my life and that something bigger and better was waiting for me as soon as I closed this door.

Taking action by not signing the contract prepared me to walk farther down my spiritual path. I listened to my inner wisdom for guidance and direction. It was an inner knowing that reached beyond any rational thought. I believe that playing music that night helped me to develop the ability to receive the message, listen to it and take action. After the show, I was presented with a test of sorts: a man with a contract worth a lot of money. Now it was time to see if I could stay true to myself and the messages that I received from my inner wisdom. I heard the voice that had appeared to me when I was a teenager, the voice that told me that if I stayed true to myself and my passion for music, I would always be taken care of.

I did not wait, and I did not hesitate. I jumped into a new reality that night. I was flying. I felt a deep sense of freedom that confused me initially. But because the feeling was euphoric, I quickly decided to leave the confusion alone. I closed the doors of that time and opened new ones that night. Now I needed to be patient to see what was next for me. Within a week, I realized I should leave Seattle. My time there had served me well, and I had learned many valuable lessons. Now it was time to begin the next chapter in my story.

CHAPTER SIX

Emotional Intelligence

◫　　　◫　　　◫

Emotional Messages

Emotions are a human's state of mind that is interacting with biochemical and environmental stimuli. Emotions serve to motivate us. They often determine what kind of action we will take in the moment or in the future. We often associate emotions with either a positive or negative sensation and tend to be easily persuaded by them and gravitate toward the positive sensation. Emotions are not sensations; they are messages, and if we have the wisdom of the Master Within we can identify and choose to respond to them in a way that is valuable to our goal of developing a deep spiritual path.

Emotional intelligence is the ability to recognize that the value in your emotions is measured by your ability to stay connected to your spirit, especially during times of stress or perceived stress. If you have emotional intelligence, you may not feel stress at all. Emotional intelligence requires the integration of gratitude, humility, forgiveness, compassion and unconditional love.

Since the beginning, we have had emotions. Our culture and the development of humankind have changed, but have our emotions kept up with the changes?

Before the industrial revolution humans lived in close-knit societies, where technological development was seen as the development of the connectivity in our relationships to other humans, mother Earth and the spiritual realms. This spiritual technology produced very evolved cultures that developed a high emotional intelligence required for an active participation with highly evolved beings from other worlds and realms. The Mayan, Incan, Hopi, Zuni, Egyptian, Ethiopian, Dogon and many others were highly evolved cultures that had developed sophisticated social structures that produced high levels of wisdom and spiritual development and demanded emotional literacy, responsibility and intelligence from society members.

The industrial revolution began to change all that. Communities began to change their priorities from sustainability to productivity. With this came the breakdown of the social structure and ultimately a profound change in the way humans developed relationships with each other, Mother Earth and the Spirit realms. More energy was directed toward a new kind of technology, the spiritual connectivity of communities was no longer sustainable and the foundation of spiritual technology began to disappear. Today we see the results of the development of this new technology. We live in a world where it is possible for us to be very comfortable in the material world. We have machines and gadgets that provide solutions for our physical needs, synthetic drugs that seem to provide solutions for our mental and emotional needs, computers that have given us the sense of connection via micro and macro networking, and books and movies that are touted as solutions for our spiritual needs.

"All things must evolve. It is the nature of the universe. Spiritual evolution is quiet and invisible, whereas technological evolution is often loud and destructive. The greater the presence of spirit, the more gentle, subtle and less polluting technological evolution will be."

– Malidoma Some

Since this shift in technology from the spiritual realm to the physical realm, we have experienced a radical shift in the perception of what our emotions are and what they offer us. Our emotions no longer are perceived to be valuable in spiritual development. Rather, they are seen as crippling, and our culture seeks to neutralize them with drugs, creating a culture that no longer recognizes the value of the messages contained in our emotions. It is time to re-connect with the idea that our emotions are important and valuable resources for our spiritual development. The spirit world and the physical world are equally dependent on each other and honor each other's existence. Our emotions offer us the possibility to live in the physical and connect to the spiritual. They are powerful tools of spiritual evolution and offer us the opportunity to find the Master Within.

The messages that our emotions give us are powerful clues to our spiritual development. Emotions tell us where we are spiritually and often point directly to the virtues we are looking to develop. For example, when we think a friend has betrayed us, we may feel the emotions of sadness, anger, jealousy and envy. These emotions point us to the virtue of forgiveness. Developing a sincere practice of forgiveness can eliminate these negative emotions and instead produce feelings of unconditional love, inner peace and serenity. However, there are steps that need to be taken in order for us to reach this place. We need to recognize that the sense of betrayal comes from within us, not the actions or words of another person. We need to recognize that it is only us who can change what we feel and think; others are not responsible for our thoughts and emotions. We need to be willing to transform our negative thoughts and emotions into positive actions toward others, especially those who we think have betrayed us. Finally, we need to take action in serving those people by helping them shift to a more positive position. We can do this by not accepting their gift of betrayal, by remaining calm, and by showing them a more positive way of dealing with the situation. Perhaps we accept the blame of their accusations, or we can offer a sincere apology for what they perceive to be regressions on our part. If we want to sincerely recognize and utilize the messages in our emotions, we will be willing to take the positive position of having nothing to protect; we will be willing to shift our perceptions to experience freedom in any situation.

Unfortunately, many of us do not know how to respond to our emotions and we make quick judgments about whether they are producing sensations that feel good in the moment. This kind of thinking is shortsighted and will ultimately lead to more negative sensations. The popular solution has been to manage our emotions, to keep them at bay so they do not have control over our behavior. This may be beneficial in the sense that we may be able to control our actions when we feel anger so that we do not hurt others, physically or emotionally. Ultimately, we want to release and let go of these negative emotions so they no longer influence our thoughts and behavior. Our culture tells us that the most emotionally intelligent people know how to embrace emotions fully. It tells us that expressing them is the only way to release them and that we must relive traumatic and painful experiences so that we are able to fully let them go. With this model, life becomes a roller coaster; we live at the whim of our emotions. We enjoy the highest of highs but experience the lowest of lows as well. There is a way we can live a more balanced emotional existence.

What if you didn't need to experience the lowest of lows? Are we so addicted to the highs that we are willing to pay the heavy price of enduring the lows? We need to arrive at a place where we stop managing our emotions and begin to take an active participation in our transformation and spiritual development. There is a middle path where one is willing to let go of the highs and the lows and experience a stable flow of contentment and joy that surpasses the best of the highs and inflicts none of the lows. This state produces a constant feeling of serenity so deep and so powerful that one will always desire to stay there. The paradox lies in the notion that if we choose to relinquish the desire to remain in a place of serenity will stay with us.

How can we change our perception of our emotions? Perceptions shape our beliefs, thoughts and actions and are deeply connected to our emotions and our level of emotional intelligence. For example, if we have the perception that we are in a struggle for respect from others, we will have a greater tendency to react negatively when we believe we have been disrespected. The perception that we are in a struggle for respect informs a belief that others disrespect us. It also produces thoughts about how others disrespect us and leads to actions that are of a defensive nature. A perception that others have no respect for us may also produce offensive actions to head off the possibility of future negative perceptions.

A greater level of emotional intelligence is developed through transforming our perceptions, beliefs, thoughts and actions. To do this, we need to look at our emotions from a more objective perspective. Instead of owning them immediately, we can make a decision to observe them and observe our reaction to them. Neuroscientific research suggests there is a "magic quarter-second" during which it's possible to catch a thought before it becomes an emotional reaction. In that moment, we can catch the emotion before allowing it to influence our thoughts and actions. (Tara-Bennett Goleman wrote a book about this idea called Emotional Alchemy: How the Mind Can Heal the Heart.) Then we can reflect about where they are coming from. Are they connected to a particular event, or have we been carrying them for many years? Are past events affecting our experience, or have we been able to completely let go of the emotions of our past? If we can manage to be more objective with our emotions, we will have the opportunity to receive the messages they hold for us.

We are spirits having a human experience that prepares our spirit for the next phase of growth. Being human gives our being tangible evidence of the state of our physical, mental, emotional and spiritual being. The human experience is a barometer of sorts. We are able to see our reflection in everyone and everything. When we develop this awareness, our spirit begins to use this powerful tool to grow in profound ways. When someone brings you anger, you may find yourself feeling angry, especially if you are the object of his or her anger. If you have no anger inside, you cannot feel anger. It is your anger that is responsible for the anger you feel. Having emotional responsibility means recognizing that the blame for any emotion you feel can never be placed outside yourself. You are responsible for your emotions and ultimately your reality.

◲   ◲   ◲

Garbology

Developing emotional intelligence is a must if you want to evolve spiritually. There are many ways we can pursue this development, but one stands out as the most powerful and effective. Learn to become a garbologist and transform your life forever! The art of "garbology" is simple, and once you step aside and remove your self from your ego, you can transform your self and be of service to others at the same time.

A garbologist is one who willingly takes the garbage of others, accepts the blame, transforms this negative energy into unconditional love and returns it to the person as a gift. The garbologist does this regardless of the "truth" so that the instigator may have an opportunity to shift from a negative to a more positive perspective. The shift may come in that moment or at a later time, when the person reflects on the situation. We should remember that there are many "truths." The accusations from the person may be the truth for him or her.

There are three steps one must take to become a garbologist. First, we must be willing to take the blame, to take others' accusations, anger, jealousy or any other negative emotion. Second, we must have the wisdom to transform negative emotions into unconditional love. Third, we must be creative when offering this transformation back to the aggressor.

In taking the blame from another, we must be willing to consider the possibility that we have nothing to defend. We must be willing to let go of the reactionary impulse to protect ourselves from the negative assault. The garbologist is willing to be insulted, shamed, or yelled at without a negative response or reaction. The garbologist must be willing to remain peaceful, calm, and serene in the moment of the perceived attack.

Transforming negative emotions into unconditional love is the role of an alchemist. We are all alchemists; we transform energy every day. This is something we do without thinking and without intention. For our everyday energy requirements, this is the perfect and most efficient system to have. However, to transform another's negative emotions into unconditional love requires a deep intention combined with detachment, forgiveness, compassion and gratitude.

The garbologist must be detached from any mental thought process, from any ego illusions and from any personal gain that may arise from the situation. The garbologist has a tremendous responsibility to keep sacred intentions for the well being of the aggressor. The garbologist must engage an open heart filled with forgiveness for the aggressor to bathe in. The garbologist should not have to use forgiveness if he or she is fully detached from the negative energy; rather, the forgiveness should be provided for the aggressor to use for himself if needed. The garbologist must infuse himself with compassion at the moment of attack. We can fill our energy being with compassion that will provide the aggressor with the opportunity to reflect and defuse the negative emotions, preparing them for transformation. The garbologist must have a deep sense of gratitude for the opportunity to be of service to another human being in this way.

When we become garbologists, we provide the aggressor the opportunity to make a significant shift in his perception. When we choose to meet the negativity with neutrality or positivity, we provide the space for a shift of consciousness in both people. There is one moment in time when the aggressor may see a reflection of what he is projecting onto the other person. He may see a reflection of what is inside himself at that moment, and he may also see what is underneath that negativity. This experience may serve to provide a deep sense of humility, calm and inner peace. The mind may experience confusion and choose to stop this negative emotional trajectory. Playing the role of the garbologist is an effective way of defusing a potentially hostile situation. The role of the garbologist is one of the most honorable ways of serving others and a mission of peace.

CHAPTER SEVEN

Creating a Balance of Energy

▣   ▣   ▣

Negotiating Harmony

Life is a delicate balance, and all living things are created with a harmonious proportion of elements and energy, elements from the physical world and energy from the invisible worlds. One of the unique aspects of being human is our ability to influence, change and manipulate this balance for better or for worse. Our perceptions inform our thoughts and provide us with a foundation for making decisions and taking action. These choices strengthen the balance or imbalance we experience in our lives. When there is balance, we experience inner peace and serenity. Imbalance creates the opportunity for discomfort and disease to exist and grow.

For most of us, finding this balance can be challenging. At times it may seem like a war, an inner conflict of positive and negative forces, each wanting control of our thoughts and actions. All of us have experienced the consequences of acting from a place of negativity. We ought to remember that there is no winning in the game of war, whether it is inside ourselves or outside in the world. The only means of ending a war is creating balance. When we create inner balance, we serve the energy we are made of, and we honor the very source of what we are.

Collectively, we are all energy and made of the same life force, and we are connected on many profound levels. Because we are human, we have the unique ability to determine where we receive our energy from and how we use it. Contentment, serenity and inner peace will provide us with the fuel we need to navigate our life in a positive and productive manner. These positive emotions originate from the source of all life, which is love. When we are getting our energy from this universal life force of love, we are connected to something infinite. When we connect to love, we are connected to a life force, an energy source that will provide us with unending motivation to love and live in a state of deep contentment and inner peace. The feeling of living in the energy of love is subtle and builds over time. Negative emotions offer us a tornado of powerful energy. Anger, frustration, sadness, jealousy and envy will provide us with short-term energy, but only enough to stay in that state. Beyond that, we are exhausted because it depletes more energy than it creates. Negative energy always takes more than it provides. The mind would rather witness a tornado than a slow gentle breeze, but if we can train our minds to accept the subtleties of love initially, we will soon observe the fullness of life that love offers.

Being happy will allow us to create a balance in our life. We are better able to flow with what may come our way and navigate life from a positive perspective. We need to create a balance of Mind, Body and Spirit in our everyday life. If we allow ourselves to get out of balance with any of these, we create negative energy. Tame the mind, invigorate the body and empower the spirit.

To create balance in your life, be your passion, align your thoughts and actions with your heart, pay attention to silence and stillness and play or listen to music that allows your spirit to fly. Music is a language that the spirit clearly understands. Listening to or playing music enables you to connect with your spirit. This direct connection allows you to access the wisdom of your spirit. Your spirit contains all the wisdom you need for experiencing balance, peace, contentment, and serenity.

Balance with Music

Playing music will provide you with a deeper connection with your spirit, but listening to music that has been infused with life-force energy can be just as effective. It can be challenging to find this kind of music. A good place to start is any indigenous and ceremonial music. Look for music that is played for more than 20 minutes without stopping. This will provide you the minimum time frame you'll need to devote to connecting with your spirit. Some of this music may sound strange or discordant to your ear, but do not judge the sound; it is created this way for a very important reason, to distract your mind and allow you to connect with your spirit. Indigenous peoples around the world are experts in connecting mind, body and spirit. The aesthetics may be strange to us at times, but this is yet another opportunity for us to expand our perceptions and boundaries so that we may see the value that music has for us in connecting with this realm.

If you are looking for music to serve this purpose, I recommend Native American powwow drumming music or solo flute music. You may want to find music with Tibetan horns and bowls or the Australian didgeridoo. Also, Africa is home to thousands of ethnicities that use ceremonial music. In addition, I have created six CDs that contain channeled life-force energy, and each has a different purpose (see the product page at the end of this book). The music is out there, and now with the world at our fingertips, the Internet makes available almost every kind of music you are looking for to help you create this balance of energy in your life.

CHAPTER EIGHT

Perception, Belief and Paradox

回   回   回

The Gift of Perception

Perception is the way we see the world and our place in it. It is the way we see ourselves in relationship to the world. We perceive the world based on our expectations. These expectations are learned within the boundaries of our own culture's perceptions. Are we looking in from the outside, or are we seeing ourselves in everything? Perceiving ourselves as being connected to all things will change the way we navigate our life. Putting this into action is beyond the mind, beyond understanding, and beyond thinking we are connected. It is an inner knowing, an inner certainty that becomes as tangible as the table I am sitting at this moment. When we begin to perceive the world with this new awareness, we place ourselves in a world of magic.

We have been given a beautiful gift of perception. It is one that can allow us to experience freedom on levels unimagined or one that allows us to think we are free as we sit in our self-made prison. It can set us free in any moment if we allow. It can take us to deep levels of awareness, oneness and unlimited love that we didn't imagine possible. It can change the core of how you navigate your life, from the most mundane activities to life-changing decisions.

Our perception is the lens through which we see the world, both seen and unseen, and forms the foundation of our beliefs, thoughts, actions, needs, wants and desires. It gives us parameters into which we place the world, the Universe and everything contained within them. It eases the mind and allows us to experience sensations, feelings, emotions, thoughts, and beliefs that reinforce a sense of security. We have learned ideas of what our reality consists of, and we associate specific actions and reactions with incoming messages that provide us with feelings and sensations. We attach judgment to these learned ideas that fit within a collective cultural philosophy and form a perception based within our learned belief system.

It is our perception of any given situation that provides us the opportunity to take action in a specific way or toward a specific destination. If we experience someone's anger toward us, oftentimes we feel attacked or threatened and take a defensive position. This position arises from a perception that we have something to protect. This perception that tells us that we must protect ourselves is the source of our actions and reactions. This perception can be changed. Shifting our perception can allow us to make decisions that offer more positive and productive outcomes.

◫   ◫   ◫

Faculties of Perception

Our faculties of perception allow us to hold perception. They are what embody our intuition, our emotions and our senses, both physical and spiritual. Our faculties of perception can be influenced by forces or interactions that are outside our physical being. These forces and interactions may dictate which faculties are being used. We can change the perception by eliminating the faculty holding it. Say our faculty of fear is holding a perception. If we eliminate the fear, the perception associated with it will also disappear. Eliminating the faculty of fear may start with a decision, a conscious choice to eradicate fear from our reality. We may use the logical mind to rationalize fear out of our existence. After we consider the possibility that fear does not exist and is an illusion of our mind, we can bring that possibility into the process of connecting to the spirit worlds, the invisible.

We may use music to make this connection, and when we do, we infuse that connection with the idea that fear is an illusion. It is like welding that idea to the process of connecting to our own spirit. We strengthen our connection to our spirit and to the experience of freedom from fear. We have weakened the faculty of fear and its ability to influence our perception. We can use music by playing an instrument or by listening to it. Either way, we should create a sacred ceremonial space for this kind of intention.

Understanding the Message

Changing our perceptions opens doors that provide us an existence full of deep happiness, contentment, peace and serenity. This change strengthens our ability to negotiate life in a more meaningful and purposeful way and provides endless opportunities to be a sincere servant to our mission with a deep sense of humility, devotion and passion.

One of the perceptions we can choose to adopt is that nothing bad ever happens! Are you kidding? Of course bad things happen, and I can tell you at least 10 things that have gone wrong in the past 24 hours! The bus driver slammed the brakes and I went crashing into the seat in front of me. And the person ahead of me at the grocery store decided to go back to retrieve something just as he was almost finished with the transaction, forcing me and four other people to wait.

There is a message in every situation and interaction. If we have the ability to perceive the message, we can shift and transform. The idea that a bad thing happened or something went wrong has foundation in our perspective and in our ability to see beyond our current perception. We should realize that our perception is not the only one available, that there are other levels of perception that embody higher levels of awareness that many humans do not engage. It is possible to have these higher levels of awareness; they are available to us always. Being open to the possibility of other perspectives is the first step in changing our perception and our ability to "see" how it is possible that nothing wrong or bad ever happens.

In these two examples, there are messages available to us. When I wrote about crashing into the seat in front of me when the bus driver slammed on the breaks, I failed to mention that in the moments before the incident, I was thinking about how things were going in my life and all the struggles I have had. It seemed as if life was just one struggle after another. Then the incident happened and it provided me confirmation that, yes indeed, life is a struggle.

The grocery-store incident was also frustrating. I was already late and convinced I would miss my appointment. I was so angry at the insensitivity of that person that I missed an opportunity to be of service to others. Maybe I could have seen a similar reaction among the others who were waiting and said something to help them shift to a more positive perception. By starting a lighthearted conversation, I may have been able to provide them an opportunity of peace. The art of distraction provides a window of transformation and is a powerful tool in helping others. The late psychiatrist Milton H. Erickson has many wise words about this subject.

The message here is a simple one: You create your own reality. You are what you think, and if you think life is a struggle, you will find yourself in situations to provide you ample opportunities for struggle. You may even project your struggle in situations that do not warrant it. I am not suggesting that you or your perceptions and projections created these incidents; rather, the universe will provide you many incidents that resonate with your intentions. If you are sincere in your desire to develop and evolve spiritually, the universe conspires to support those intentions. It may be the case that things around you do not change. You still had the bus accident and the experience at the store, but your perception shifted so much that you no longer experienced them as negative or bad. Change your perceptions and you will change your reality.

The art of walking a spiritual path is a practice and requires diligence, determination and patience. Engaging the path with deep devotion, passion and dedication will offer more beautiful gifts than one could ever imagine. Focus on the path and keep your eyes on the prize. There will be plenty of distractions available, and I assure you, all of them lead to drama. Leave the drama to those who choose to travel with the illusions of the mind.

As each moment passes, we are in the now, the present. Or are we? We have the perception that life is moving so fast. Actually, it is. Time is moving faster than in the past, both physically and in our perception, but that is another book. I will not go into that here, but I encourage you to look into it further. My point is that it is difficult to change perception when you are living in the past or the future. Many people spend so much time negotiating the past and the future that they miss out on the present moment, where the doors of perception wait for them. The present moment holds everything, the past and the future, along with our faculties of perception. Being in the present moment is having the experience of oneness with All That Is and offers us the opportunity to exist in harmony with everything. There is no struggle in the present moment, only freedom, contentment and inner peace.

▣　　　▣　　　▣

A Belief Is Not a Truth

Our beliefs influence our perception. Our beliefs are a collection of ideas and concepts that we have placed judgments on and attached "truths" to. And individual belief systems are connected to a community's beliefs. They are based in a collective consciousness that exists within a specific cultural paradigm. They are systems of thought we have learned, and they form the foundation of our perceptions. Every thought we experience and every action we execute has a foundation in our belief system. Western modernity does not adequately prepare us to walk a spiritual path. The collective belief system dictates a reality where we carry self-doubt and are subject to negative emotions such as anger, sadness, jealousy, and impatience.

We perceive the world based on our expectations. Therefore, transforming our belief system can be painful and uncomfortable. We expect that enlightenment is available to only those who meditate or lead a solitary life in a monastery. We expect that life will be full of disappointments or that we must do everything ourselves because relying on others will always fail. There are so many expectations that limit our beliefs. Moving from a limited to an unlimited belief system can be smooth if we surrender to nonlinear thinking. We need to step away from the mind and the perceptions it creates that strengthen our limited beliefs. We need to step into a perception that we embody more than just our mind; we embody both the physical and spiritual realms.

Expanded Perception

Deepening our spiritual path means we must expand our perceptions so we may experience ourselves in the unseen or spiritual realms. So much of what occurs in the invisible is not accessible by the mind alone. Our belief system is constructed with our eyes, ears and language.

We should engage these worlds with spiritual senses. We see with our eyes, but we should strive to see with our inner eyes, which see beyond the veil of this reality. We hear with our ears, but we should strive to listen to the silence and guidance within. Learning to see with our spiritual eyes is a product of expanded perceptions and a transformed belief system. If we want to expand or change our perceptions, we must transform our belief system.

Changing our belief system means inventing, shaping and reformulating our codes of living and our experiences and provides us the opportunity to transform our perceptions and, in turn, change our thoughts and actions. We need to reformulate our questions and stay clear of fixing problems and treating symptoms. We have been asking "why" since we were children. We always want to know how things got to be the way they are. We are curious as to the reasoning behind a comment, a rule or a thought. The spiritual path is often full of paradoxes that cannot be observed from this kind of linear perspective. When we begin to ask questions that do not point to the past but point to the present and the future, we will have begun a path of transformation. Instead of asking "why," we should ask "what for," "how," and "when." Try this for a month: Every time you catch yourself asking "why," stop and ask "what for," "how," and "when." You will find that the way you think about life will begin to shift, you will begin to observe your beliefs objectively and this will provide you the opportunity to transform them. Transform your beliefs and you will change your perceptions. Change your perceptions and you will know how to create your own reality. The world is yours to enjoy, honor, and serve with humility, detachment and gratitude.

Most people think in terms of their native language, which embodies a perspective of the world that sets forth its liberties and limitations. We should strive to think in metaphors and poems, where the rules are easily changed and other realities are accessible. We will become aware of the paradoxes of the spiritual path. Rumi, the Sufi mystic and poet, has a way to describe the spiritual realms and help change and expand our perception with only words. I have been reading Rumi for years, but it wasn't until I began walking a deeper path myself that I began to understand how Rumi experiences the spiritual worlds. For so long, I read his words of being drunk with love; I read as he described waiting for the moment to jump into another reality and without hesitation, melting with the lover who would take him there. It was then that I realized the lover was himself. He became the phenomenon. Most of us look forward just to the experience of a spiritual event. We are trained to think that the experience is the most we could hope for. Many of us reach that experience and then spend many years having a love affair with the memory of it or longing for another moment when the time is right.

Expanded Beliefs

Your beliefs can provide you a deep sense of either freedom or oppression. Our beliefs often dictate how we respond to external stimuli. For example, sometimes it can be very wise to choose to be happy rather than to be "right." For many, our culture has taught us that it is important to be right or that it is important to impose our moral judgments on others. We are often caught in the trap of thinking that our way is the only right way and that others should also abide by our perception. We have all been in situations where we had the option of choosing to either defend and propagate our beliefs or respect others' beliefs and not impose our own. Sometimes, engaging in such a debate leads us into a defensive position, and if we are emotionally attached to our beliefs, this may lead us into a place of feeling betrayed or inferior. These are all feelings of oppression. Ironically, they originate from inside us, although we may blame the other person for the life we give these feelings. Often it may be best to step back and allow others to have their perceptions and beliefs without imposing ours onto the conversation or onto the person. This position offers us freedom from emotional oppression and engages a practice of tolerance, patience and even compassion. When we practice walking a deep spiritual path, we allow others to have their beliefs, perspectives and perceptions. It does not matter if we agree. We are more interested in cultivating inside what is needed to reach the highest state of awareness possible than in defending any belief or perception we have.

Beliefs can be limiting or unlimited. Below are some examples of limited and unlimited beliefs.

Intimacy

Limited Belief: Intimacy requires two people and is experienced through emotional connection and physical sensation. There has always been a heavy price to pay for this kind of intimacy: drama, emotional roller-coaster rides from extreme highs to extreme lows. Our emotional state is dependent on the other person.

Unlimited Belief: Intimacy is experienced in solitude and is another tool to facilitate our experience as a spiritual being. When we are in a state of intimacy, we can be more effective in doing the work we are here to do. Intimacy with another human is the aligning and melting of our energy centers. This can be done with or without physical intimacy and should always have pure intention as the motivation.

Cultivating intimacy with our Spirit is at the core of developing a spiritual path. We have been taught very specific ideas and beliefs about what intimacy is and how to get it. Most of the time, we seek intimacy from others and confuse love and desires for physical contact with intimacy. We look outside ourselves to complete the connection within ourselves. Cultivating an inner sense of intimacy is paramount to knowing who we are.

Who Am I?

Limited Belief: I am someone who wants to help others, but I am limited by the system of beliefs that this physical reality and this culture impose on me. It is difficult to take care of others and myself at the same time.

Unlimited Belief: I am a spirit who has chosen to take a human body to carry out the mission of helping the Great Awakening happen in a smooth way. I am not limited to the laws of this physical world. My body is a hologram of who I am. I am immune to suffering as soon as I recognize myself. I am like a plant rooted in the soil of the ocean but free to sway with the ocean currents as they come, or like a tree rooted in the earth but also flexible to sway in the wind.

▣　　　▣　　　▣

The Paradoxes of the Path

Multiple paradoxes often envelop the spiritual path. A paradox is a statement or group of statements that leads to a contradiction or a situation that defies intuition; or it can be an apparent contradiction that actually expresses a non-dual truth. Our thoughts are verbal formulas we create to make sense of our experiences. In the West, we have been trained in linear, or cause-and-effect, thinking. This means we are trained to look at things in a very linear and logical fashion. Our perception is limited to placing ideas and concepts into a framework that produces seemingly rational solutions for most problems. The idea of the problem is not to be changed; it is a static idea. Within the framework of cause-and-effect thinking, the solution becomes the focus of the thought process.

Circular thinking allows for the idea of the problem and even the idea that a problem exists to bring us to the focal point of the thought process. It encourages us to take a look at our perceptions and beliefs and decide what is important and evaluate our priorities. Most Eastern and indigenous cultures embrace life with circular concepts that provide a different way of perceiving the world. They show us the world metaphors, anecdotes and stories. Circular thinking allows us to change our beliefs and perceptions and unravel the paradoxes of a spiritual path and the mysteries of life.

We would be wise to consider the notion that we do not understand the full extent of these paradoxes and we do not need to understand them to walk a deep path. Understanding the spiritual path is always on a need-to-know basis, and more often than not, we do not need to know. Given that, we are always granted access to understanding after we have let go of the desire for such understanding and have taken action without understanding the process and the outcome.

Despite this knowledge, the desire for spiritual growth is accompanied by the desire to understand the concepts before taking action. This a paradox in that when we attempt to put the perceptions of the spiritual path into the framework of the student's belief systems, we create a situation that cannot be understood, and the student will often perceive that he or she cannot proceed until it is understood. The reality is that the need to understand is not necessary when walking a spiritual path. The desire to understand has a foundation in the past when the student seeks to move forward. Remaining focused on moving forward regardless of the current perceptions of non-understanding will ultimately provide the student with a new level of perception and understanding that embodies a broader perspective to include a new and deeper level of awareness.

I have been calling my teachers/mentors "the masters of confusion" for many years now. Seems that most times I think I understand something, I realize it was not as it appeared. The art of asking circular questions enables the student to observe his or her perspective and belief systems in a way that provides space for deep reflection and transformation that originates from within. The primary obstacle to finding our inner wisdom is self-doubt. When we have self-doubt, we are unable to act in a meaningful and purposeful way. Our perception becomes a slave to self-doubt and is limited. For many, self-doubt is a permanent existence and can be difficult to let go of, especially when the desire to understand is the foundation of the doubt. The way to release doubt is through a deep sense of humility, patience, tolerance, compassion and forgiveness. When we are willing to let go of who we think we are, we release our perceived expectations and limitations regarding ourselves and allow for a deep sense of freedom that provides us with an inner knowing that is beyond doubt.

One of my students has been cultivating a deep practice of using the drum to travel to other dimensions and be of service to humans and Mother Earth. He is captivated by the idea that we are able to travel to other dimensions to be of service. He comes to me with this problem: He is never convinced that he is doing anything. He tells me he cannot remember if he went anywhere or did anything. He is always asking me how he can know he is making a difference in his sessions. Seems like a reasonable question, and for someone who is living and trained in the linear thinking of the Western world, it is not only reasonable but also required to understand the idea within the context. For the occidental mind, it is impossible to experience the action in another dimension without a preconceived perception of what that action will look like and feel like. The occidental mind requires this so that it has something to measure the experience by. Unfortunately, the rules of the occidental mind are what destroy the ability to perceive the action in other dimensions. Until we are able to let go of the desire for understanding, we will not experience the subtleties of the spiritual world.

The awareness that is required to perceive other dimensions is available to us and is dependent on our ability to detach from the occidental mind and from linear thinking and perceptions. My student will become aware of what he is doing in these other dimensions when he stops asking such questions. He will stop asking these kinds of questions when he stops trying to place non-linear events and actions within a linear framework. Actions in other dimensions reside outside our linear thinking and world views. It is up to us to come to them on their terms. It is we who have to rearrange our perceptions to include other dimensions. It is we who must learn how to perceive these worlds and negotiate them appropriately. It is unreasonable for us to expect to fit them within a world view that asks, "How will I know?"

He asks, "Is there a technique I can practice to achieve this awareness?" Yes, there is a technique. Well, it's not a technique per se. It is a position you hold—a faculty of perception that you cultivate and an awareness you develop. It is a complete and sincere surrender to the notion that you are not your body and that you are a part of something called Love, which embodies more than your linear reality provides you. It requires that you be willing to die to everything you desire to serve. Right now, at this moment, it requires that you are ready to leave the Earth if needed. It is a complete willingness to consider the possibilities that reside outside your current perception and a deep desire to be of service to the Great Spirit and the Masters in other dimensions. This practice can be approached with curiosity, humility and gratitude as you allow the world of magic to envelop you as you melt with your inner being.

▣   ▣   ▣

Redefining Trust and Love

There are many layers of perception and belief. As we peel away each layer, we expose another that is deeper and more ingrained. These are the beliefs that are less obvious and need transformation. They are the foundation of our perceived reality and include strict definitions of concepts we use to define the parameters of our existence. These layers include concepts such as trust and love. Culturally, we have defined these concepts as "truths" and assigned them a sort of sacred meaning that defines a sense of normalcy within the culture.

Many people consider trust to be one of the most valuable truths we have. We use the faculty of trust everyday. Our perception of whether we are able to trust often forms the foundation of our thoughts and actions. It determines if we are able to be generous, vulnerable, intimate, outgoing or personable, and it tells us if we should be protective, guarded, closed, or stingy. Trust is one of the core tools we use to navigate our path in this life. Trust is unneeded and archaic. Trust is perceived as useful only to those who have not remembered how to love completely and unconditionally.

Tell me, what is the foundation of trust? What idea or concept is at the heart of a decision that utilizes trust? Why is it that we desire to utilize trust? Seems to me that we fear something or that we desire to protect ourselves or maintain some level of security. Trust is used to try to protect, ensure or strengthen a belief we have developed. When we lose the desire to protect a belief and strengthen our sense of security, we can begin to use a more powerful tool than trust will offer us. We will then be able to develop a deep awareness that will provide us with the inner knowing required to make better decisions. The tool I am referring to is Wisdom. Utilizing our inner Wisdom trumps trust. Trust becomes unnecessary and obsolete. So, trust can be a truth that we use, and it will provide us a certain level of comfort until we begin injecting our beliefs with illusions and projecting them onto others. Then trust becomes our enemy. It is no longer useful in our goal of feeling secure and protecting our belief. Trust is a truth that will not serve us in walking a spiritual path.

Love is another truth that we have twisted into some strange monster that allows us to slowly destroy ourselves and others. Culturally, we have managed to mutilate the sacred virtue of love into a potent cocktail of fear, jealousy, envy and anger. We carry this sack of negative emotions around and unleash it on our closest and most intimate relationships whenever our idea of love is not being honored. We have placed the idea of love within a framework of linear thinking, and we have thrown in a good dose of trust to keep it firmly in place within the boundaries of fear. We have forgotten that love is the foundation of all existence. Love is what we are all made of. Love is what we participate in. It is not something we are able to use within a rational thought process developed by the mind to protect itself from the illusion of pain.

⧉   ⧉   ⧉

The Affliction of the Mind

What a corner we have gotten ourselves into. We have allowed our minds to run the show. We have allowed our minds to create the rules, the parameters within which we perceive the world and develop beliefs that are the basis of our actions. The mind has created an elaborate system of layers designed to keep what it perceives to be "outside forces"—anything originating outside itself—from taking over. Ironically, this means that our innate desire to seek out an inner meaning and define the purpose of life and our existence as human is carried out by looking to the outside world, the physical world and anything and everything outside ourselves.

Walking a spiritual path requires us to recognize the affliction that the mind can produce; it requires that we begin to look inward and develop a relationship with our inner being. The road to our inner being is created with detachment, forgiveness, and gratitude. The road is laid on a bed of music that moves our awareness toward a deeper realization of the self, who we are, what our purpose is here and how we are going to take our path. Music provides us a beautiful way to perceive and interpret our inner journey. Music is unbiased and offers us a pure reflection of our inner being. This is because music is not of the mind but can surround the mind and soothe it into relaxation and eradicate any resistance it may have.

Our Spiritual Senses

Learning how to use our mind allows us the opportunity to engage our senses in new ways and explore the possibilities of new senses we were not aware of. We have five senses that allow us to perceive the physical world. Each sensory organ provides us stimuli that we interpret and use for decision-making and navigating the world around us. Our eyes provide us a perception of the physical world, and this allows us to easily navigate and enjoy the beauty of the natural world. Our ears provide us the faculty of listening to the natural world, music and the voice of others. Our nose offers us the possibility of smell and the opportunity to partake in all the scents of the earthly world. Our tongues are the home of taste buds, which allow us to taste everything we put in our mouths. Finally, our skin offers us the sense of touch, which allows us to enjoy the many textures of the physical world.

I cannot imagine being human without these senses, as they form the foundation of the development of our perceptions of the physical world. We should be careful in making the assumption that these senses provide us with absolute knowledge. Our physical senses offer us one possibility of perception; they are not providing us with absolute information but rather telling us that this perception is a starting place for our perceptions. They offer us variations in themes and at no point give us any interpretation or judgments. Our physical senses are always neutral. They work in collaboration with the rational mind to provide a foundation for a decision to take action. Our senses provide us neutral interpretations of events in the physical world, and our mind interprets them, applies judgments and informs our muscles to take action. For example, when we smell something that our rational mind interprets to be toxic or dangerous to our body, we will take action to remove ourselves from the situation or context that is producing the perceived danger.

Our physical senses offer us a perception that extends to the physical world, whereas our humanness offers us additional senses that offer alternate perceptions of the physical and nonphysical worlds. These cosmic senses tell us of our past and can give us previews of the future. These senses provide us opportunities to perceive ourselves in the context of our cosmic memory and tell us who we are, where we have come from and what our mission is here in this body. Our cosmic memory is the realization of the self, the true identity of who we are and the recognition of one's own spirit. These cosmic senses are internal senses that aid us in the practice and process of awakening. They point our attention inward and lead our awareness deep into our inner being. Developing our cosmic senses is essential in awakening the inner being.

For example, we can utilize the ideas of some of the physical senses to help up understand the cosmic senses. Our spiritual eyes allow is to "see" through the veil of the physical realm and perceive the magic of the spiritual realms. Our spiritual eyes are connected to our intuition and imagination. We need to remember how to use these eyes in a deep and meaningful way. We can use music to help us see with our spiritual eyes. Music is sound waves that can provide an opening for our awareness to enter other dimensions. We can use music to remember how to see through the veil of the physical world. When you engage your spiritual eyes when listening to music, it may be helpful to close your eyes. Now look at the music with your spiritual eyes. What do you see? What color is it? What shape is it? How big or small is it. Does it have a beginning or an end?

Our spiritual ears provide us a true and unbiased perception of the sounds of the spiritual realms. When we begin to listen with our spiritual ears, we hear the wisdom of the Master within, and wisdom is transformed into action as it moves from the spiritual to the physical realm. Music is also a perfect vehicle for beginning to remember how to listen to your inner being. Music bypasses the mind and allows us to enter into our inner worlds and to listen to the wisdom of our inner being. When we listen with our spiritual ears, we listen through the sound, not to the sound. When we listen to music, we listen through the music. This implies that we need to become the music. We need to melt with the music in such a way that we experience time and space as music, that we embody the consciousness of music, which means we become All That Is, or the source of all life. We are life when we when we listen with spiritual ears.

Our taste buds provide us the pleasure (or displeasure) of experiencing the many flavors of food around the world. Spiritually, our sense of taste allows us to experience the flavors of cosmic food that nurtures our entire being. When listening to music, melt completely with it and consume it fully. What does the music taste like? Is it bitter, tangy, zesty or sweet? You may discover some taste sensations you never experienced before.

Our sense of smell enhances life in ways most if us take for granted, and the opportunity to experience the physical world with smell is often overlooked. Our spiritual sense of smell is also important to our experience the spirit worlds, and we can use music to help us explore this beautiful sense. Does the music smell like a fresh-cut lawn, a flowery meadow or a puffy cloud? Engage your spiritual sense of smell and embrace a new perception and experience.

The human skin is one of the most important organs of the body. Our skin is a bridge between our bodies and the spiritual and the material worlds. Physically, it serves as a protective barrier, keeping our bodies safe from outside intrusions. Spiritually, our skin provides us access to other realms of the Spirit and holds secrets of the Universe and our mission on Earth. It connects us to our ancestors and contains messages from the past, present and future. We can use our skin to connect, expand and melt with the realm of the spirit. We can use music to access a place where we dissolve our physical body and where we melt with sound. Our skin expands and we recognize it as the fabric of the universe. We are one, we are everything and we are nothing. How does your skin feel when it comes into contact with music? What happens to your physical being when music envelops it?

CHAPTER NINE

The Role of Community

回   回   回

The Community and Consciousness

What is the role of community awareness and collective consciousness? How does the community affect our thinking and awareness? Does a community create its reality? How can we choose our reality while living in this culture? How does our culture support its members?

In many indigenous and traditional societies, the principal task of community is to create balance within the individual and the relationships among community members. The priority of the individual is the health of the community because he knows that if the community is healthy, its members are also more likely to be healthy. Likewise, if the community is unhealthy, it is more likely that the community members will also become unhealthy. The first question of a person participating in a community should be "How can I best serve others?" Service is the fabric of community; the role of the individual is always to be in service to the community.

In return, the community will support its members. How should a community support its members? A healthy community recognizes the value of the individual and is in service to that individual. The community places value on the acceptance and tolerance of all individuals within the community and supports the priorities set forth in the collective consciousness. All our perceptions are products of our relationships. The way we are in relationship is constructed by our participation in our community, which is informed by our culture.

Western and occidental cultures perceive community in a different way. For the West, community is present to support us in whatever cause or agenda we bring to it.

Generally speaking, a Western culture does not support community. Rather, it expects a community to support the individual when the individual has identified himself with an idea that needs the support of others to grow.

Western cultures have developed an elaborate hierarchy of communities within communities. In certain circumstances, academic and scientific communities have created specific ideas of normalcy that the larger community then embraces. The culture of psychology has developed a truth regarding psychological disorders and has given names to conditions that reside outside the cultural and community definition of normalcy. This creates a situation where those who are labeled with such conditions are taught to create change or transformation to align them selves with the cultural norm. The institution of psychology is defined within the cultural values and limits definitions of normalcy to those of the culture. For many conditions, this is inadequate.

If we look beyond our culture, we will find a vast history of context for the suggested disorder. One culture's disorder is another culture's gift. For some cultures, these conditions serve a purpose and are held in high regard. For example, in many cultures the condition we call schizophrenia is seen as a gift. The person who has been diagnosed with schizophrenic symptoms may be seen as an intermediary between the physical and spiritual realms. With proper training, this person can live a productive life and serve the community in significant ways.

Community can ease the pain that comes with spiritual awakening. In indigenous cultures, the individual and the community feed each other in purpose. The individual cannot carry out his purpose without the community, and the community cannot exist in purpose without the individual. The health and well being of the individual is connected to the community and cannot be maintained alone or outside the community. A healthy community does not seek to change the person but rather seeks to create an environment in which the person can thrive, respond and change himself. The community's role is to create an environment that provides people the opportunity to have a meaningful experience at their level of participation.

We in the West need to be willing to step out of our modern definitions of community so that we can make the necessary changes to transform into our purpose. The reality of community in the West is one of a narrow focus on individualism and consumption, and this breeds negative and unproductive emotions that hinder our spiritual growth. Stress and emotional and mental illnesses are often a direct result of the loss of community. It can feel necessary to remove yourself from the community to restructure your belief system into one that is more conducive to spiritual growth. This is our challenge, to develop and walk a deep spiritual path while being bombarded with messages that tell us we ought to be looking outside ourselves for meaning, purpose, happiness, contentment and joy.

▣   ▣   ▣

Expanding Our Perspective

Only when we step away from our cultural and societal beliefs can we be truly objective. Our current set of tools comprises those that are used within the parameters of our Western society and are ineffective outside this culture and inoperable on the spiritual path. We need to be able to access a new set of tools for this path, and we need ways to step outside our cultural paradigms into a more expanded and unlimited perception of the self, the world, the universe and our relationship to them.

Music offers us a beautiful path to this kind of divine wisdom. The expanded perceptions that reside outside our own cultural paradigms exist for all of us. They have been there since the beginning of the human race and are waiting for us to return to them. Music has been a primary means for accessing this sacred wisdom, this collective consciousness. It is not coincidence that every group, society, and culture has music dedicated to the spiritual, dedicated to the practice of connecting to something bigger and yet something that we are a part of. Music is used to connect to the source of who we are. Music is used to connect us to each other. Music is the fabric of the human race that connects all of us. Music unifies, calms, and befriends us. Music is a peacekeeper and creates harmony. It is said that people who sing, dance and play music together will never fight. Music shows us a path of Love. How can we fight when we are busy falling in love?

CHAPTER TEN

Music, Ceremony and Ritual

▣   ▣   ▣

Music, ceremony and ritual are important tools we can use to help us implement and maintain a spiritual path. Playing music allows the mind to quiet and offers us a direct connection to our spirit and our heart. Ceremony and Ritual offers us opportunities to develop discipline and patience and provides us a connection to our own devotion, passion and desire to walk deeper. Using music and ceremony together is a powerful recipe for success when integrating a spiritual path into your life.

What is the difference between Ceremony and Ritual? This is an interesting question that deserves a few words. Ceremonies are events that are used to create and maintain our connection to the Spirit realms. They are activities and tools of change and transformation that allow us to access energies that can heal our spiritual, mental, and emotional bodies. Ceremony offers us the opportunity to move out or let go of the old to allow for new awareness to move in. It is dancing with spirit and is a powerful tool for maintaining balance between the body and the soul. It is a way to stimulate healing needed by the individual and the community.

Rituals are the actions that take place within the context of a ceremony. When we request permission to open the four directions, or when we set the candles in a particular way that is determined by the kind of ceremony we are engaged in, or when we use the drum at a particular time for a specific length of time or even play a specific rhythm—these are all examples of the anatomy of a ritual. Humans have been using ritual for thousands of years; it is in our beings, and we use it every day in very common behaviors, some with positive results and some with negative results. Ritual outside of ceremony is not functional and often will take on negative consequences for the individual performing it. It is the ritual being used in combination with our intentions within a ceremonial context that gives the ritual meaning and power.

There are two categories of ceremony. They are healing ceremonies and maintenance ceremonies. Healing ceremonies can be used to release negative or stagnant energy to make room for a more productive and positive energy and are performed when there is a need to heal a community member spiritually, emotionally, mentally or physically. Unconditional love is always the active ingredient in healing ceremonies. Participating in unconditional love optimizes the body's ability to prevent disease related to energetic imbalances such as stress and anxiety.

A maintenance ceremony is one we can do daily to maintain our connection with spirit. The purpose can vary from thanking Spirit for guidance in our life to practicing for awakening to self-mastery, creating a deeper awareness of gratitude, forgiveness, humility, serenity, and unconditional love. This will awaken within us new ways of perceiving ourselves, others and the world. Maintenance ceremonies are often done on a regular basis to help remind us that we are connected and to create the time needed to cultivate a deep spiritual path. We must always remember that it is the practice that we are after, not the end result. The result will never come if we are continually looking for it. We should be content with the practice and enjoy each moment, no matter what judgments the mind may attach to it.

Ceremonies can be done individually or in community. Community ceremonies are more effective if all members are involved and have participated in their own individual ceremonies, creating a personal connection with Spirit. Within community ceremonies, all members present should be actively participating; a passive observer will drain the energy of the group. That does not mean all members need to be physically active during the ceremony. I have attended many ceremonies where there is someone who appears to be passive but is actually negotiating spirits and energy that have come to the ceremony. That is often the most important role in a community ceremony and is assigned to someone who is at an advanced level.

We need to remember and be very clear that whatever the result of the ceremony, we are certain that we are not the cause. It is not I who heals, it is the powers from the outer worlds, and it is the Masters and Great Spirit who use us as a vehicle for healing. There is a prayer by Chief Black Elk of the Oglala Sioux that reflects this intention.

> "*I cured with the power that came through me. Of course, it was not I who cured, it was the power from the Outer World. The visions and the ceremonies had only made me like a hole through which the power could come to the two-legged. If I thought that I was doing it myself, the hole would close up and no power could come through. Then everything I could do would be foolish.*"

Our participation requires us to be extremely humble with our position, to be sincere with our intentions and to honor all energy and all spirits, what we perceive to be positive and negative, light and dark, good and evil. Positive and negative are the sides of a single coin, and one cannot exist without the other. We do not fear anything; we honor and respect the role of all beings, for we know each is doing what it was created to do.

Prepare the space for ritual. The space should look mysterious and beautiful. The goal is to prepare the psyche to move into magic and leave behind the mundane reality of everyday life. There should be a gateway to the ritual space; a doorway or hallway is good. If the space is outdoors, more effort should be made to make the gateway and the ritual space clear.

Using the natural elements— earth, fire, water, air — and other natural objects allows us to connect to nature and Mother Earth and create another bridge between the physical and spiritual realms. Symbols of the forces in the universe are also powerful objects in ritual. These can be of our own creation or actual objects from outer space. You may include a small personal object of each person to remind him of his connection to the creator and the ritual.

Next, do the invocation. A prayer that formally invites Spirit to join the ritual is recommended. I use a prayer requesting the permit to open the four directions. This request speaks to the energies that reside in each of the four directions, along with Mother Earth and Father Sky. This acts as a beacon to all beings that may be called to serve in the ritual in a positive and supportive way. The opening prayer needs to clearly state the intention of the ritual.

The heart of the ritual may be healing, cleansing, protection, freedom, and liberation. Whatever the intention of the ritual, one thing must be clear: your undivided attention to the task at hand. Ritual is a powerful way of connecting to the Spirit realm to manifest transformation in the physical realm. It is not we humans who dictate the transformation, it is Spirit who ultimately concedes to or denies whatever outcome we desire. We are humble servants to Spirit, and it is our sincerity and our willingness to serve that allow for the dance with Spirit to take place.

The closing consists of a simple and sincere expression of gratitude to Spirit. A simple statement regarding feeling gratitude for all the opportunities to change and transform that this life allows is sufficient. Of course, we can be as elaborate as we desire.

▣   ▣   ▣

The Elements

Mother Earth grounds us and connects to the root of our humanness. Mother Earth represents unconditional and unlimited love and the nurturing of life. Fire opens the door to other realms and is an eye to the Spirit world and allows us to communicate with other lives, past, present and future. Water purifies our spirit, lends authenticity to our experience and allows us to maintain the consciousness that connects us to other worlds. Water represents reconciliation, cleansing and vitality. Air connects us to inner wisdom and to the breath of life. Air represents intention and conscious communication. Earth offers us unconditional love and support and represents inclusion and healing. Mineral and stone offer us connection to our cosmic memory, creativity, stories and symbolism and allow us to remember our origins and receive messages from other worlds. Nature offers us the opportunity for change, transformation, mutation, flexibility, death and magic.

Many people create a permanent sacred space either inside or outside their living space. Altars are powerful symbols of connection to the spirit realms and can be used as tools for us to maintain that connection. Some are created to remember a loved one or deity, to be a reminder, or to show appreciation. The process of building the altar brings the builder to a place of communication with the intention. Items used to create an altar are unique, just as the creator is, but often contain objects that contain significant meaning to the person. These items are placed on a formal space designated as sacred. Altars can have different purposes and can be placed in public or private spaces. Many cultures use an altar outside the front door to protect the home from negative energy. Other cultures use altars in more private spaces, such as a bedroom or living room, for the purpose of connecting to relatives who have passed on. Many indigenous cultures use an altar room for that sole purpose.

▣   ▣   ▣

Symbols and Symbolism

Rituals and ceremonies often contain the use of symbols and symbolism as tools to connect to the spirit realm. Symbols are objects the human psyche is able to deposit and receive meaning from. They are objects that represent the spirit realms. Symbols are powerful representations of our intentions, humility, dedication and passion for the actions within a sacred context. Symbols can be anything with meaning and may include candles, crystals, feathers, stones, a photo, animal skin, the drum or any instrument, costumes or special items such as a necklace or bracelet. The use of symbols and symbolism in ritual and ceremony is important and should not be overlooked when seeking a connection with the divine.

Additionally, it should be stated here that music is acoustic symbolism, audible symbols that represent specific levels of awareness and other dimensions. The use of music in ceremony and ritual is essential to the function and experience of connecting to the spiritual realms.

Our analytical minds can easily doubt and explain the experience of healing through ceremony. Self-doubt is one of the most debilitating conditions to have when walking a spiritual path. You have everything you need inside your being. Search for direction and answers inside your soul. Searching outside ourselves will always lead to more of the same experiences we have already had. A good mentor or teacher can help by reminding us to search inward.

CHAPTER ELEVEN

Integrating A Spiritual Path Through Music

▣　　　▣　　　▣

The Message of Music

The core of any spiritual path will contain elements such as the development and practice of compassion, humility, forgiveness, gratitude and a willingness to be of service to others. How you choose to navigate the path will determine how deep you travel within it. Your current belief system has gotten you to where you are now. If you are happy where you are, don't change it. As they say, "If it isn't broken, don't fix it." However, if you are not satisfied with all aspects of your life, you may need to change the way you see the world and your participation in it. This can be as difficult or as easy as you choose. The more you are willing to detach from your desires and expectations, the easier this process will be. Likewise, the more you hold on to your present perspective and try to place it on top of new teachings and lessons, the more uncomfortable and difficult it will be.

Integrating the path means transferring all operations from your mind to your heart. The mind contains your current beliefs and perspectives and offers you a foundation from which you make decisions and take action. However, the mind contains a very limited perspective on life and the rules or laws we have created to form the parameters within which we operate. Every day we think and say things that keep us stuck in our present perceptions. Our present perception creates more of itself. If we change our perception to one that facilitates a deep awakening, that perception will also create more of itself.

A deep spiritual path requires a dismantling of the rules, laws and perspectives of the logical mind. We can do this by exploring the paradoxes of the spiritual path and turning our perceptions upside down. For example, a friend of mine recently said his current job situation is destroying the meaning of life because it makes him worry and therefore he no longer enjoys it. In reality, it is not his job situation that is destroying the meaning of life; it is his worry. The worry he experiences is prohibiting him from enjoying his job. He attributes the worry to an aspect of his job, but really, if he dropped the worry, he would have a better chance of enjoying it, or at least he could better see the opportunity in the situation.

The universe provides us clues and messages regarding our path, and it is up to us to recognize, interpret and implement them. Doing this with the mind will always lead us astray. Rather, we need to spend time in reflection and contemplation to learn to receive the messages accurately. Listen with your heart, your inner knowing and your intuition. Practice this daily and soon you will recognize the difference between the knowing of the mind and the knowing of the heart.

We are caught in the crossfire in the Western culture. Our heart and spirit want nothing more than freedom, but our mind would love nothing more than to be consumed by the distractions of external stimuli. We need to develop patience and forgiveness for ourselves and allow ourselves to make mistakes with a deep passion and devotion to continue walking and moving forward. So many people are stuck in a reality of fear of failure. They are afraid to change anything that may result in the perception of failure, so they remain in a situation that is uncomfortable but does not require the perceived risk of failure. There is no such thing as failure when we walk a spiritual path. Failure is an illusion of the mind and exists only in the academic and scientific worlds. The spiritual realms contain transformation, change, negotiation and balance. Failure is an illusion and is most often attached to fear.

One of my students recently told me he is frustrated that he cannot learn the music that he set out to learn. He is upset that he fails at reaching his own standard and thinks he may never be successful with his music. I told him he has no right to set the standard, because he has been playing music for less than a year and is not qualified to set the standard. I told him I am his teacher and the one to set the standards. I went on to say that musically, he has exceeded any standard that I could have set for him but that if he wants to become a good musician he should practice smiling more when he makes mistakes. I told him there is a standard of enjoyment that he is not meeting.

My student is learning how to find more kindness, inner peace, generosity, patience and love while learning how to play a musical instrument. The messages are in the process, the practice and the music. Music. What is it? How does it reach the deepest part of our soul? How can we receive inspiration from it? How can it make us feel deep emotions? Music resides in a place deep within us that is protected from the constructs of the mind. Music is a part of the metaphor, the anecdotes and the stories. When we listen to or play music, we become part of the story. We are free to leave the mundane world and allow our spirit to fly. When we play music, we have the opportunity to write and rewrite our story. We are free to consider, dream and live the possibilities. Maybe, just maybe, we will see that the dream is here and now and that the possibilities are endless.

We can infuse music with pure intentions of gratitude, compassion, forgiveness, humility and unconditional love, which are all powerful tools that can provide the opportunities for spiritual awakening. Playing music is an active meditation and allows the mind to relax and open a space within us that provides opportunities for deep reflection, a deep sense of surrender and freedom. Music has been used as a connection to our cosmic memory and a powerful tool to connect with the spirit worlds. When we play or listen to music, we create, strengthen and maintain this connection. We remember who we are, and we offer ourselves the opportunity to conspire with the Great Spirit to be a servant to humanity, the Earth and spirits.

Learning music will help us develop positive character attributes that demonstrate wisdom and humility. In an indigenous context, elders demonstrate their wisdom and humility when playing music. They are the ones who are able to let the other instruments speak; they are able to be free without dominating or ignoring the other rhythms, and they are able to use their insight to instigate interactions that produce meaningful communication and participation. They demonstrate character by knowing the limitations of participation; they have mastered the art of mediation and control their participation in relationship to an organized structure of relationships. They are masters of responsible involvement and communication.

□　　　□　　　□

The Power of the Drum

I have been a musician all my life. It is easy for me to tell you to learn the language of an instrument and enjoy the path of enlightenment while playing music. Many of you either have convinced yourself that you cannot learn music or that it is just not your thing. That is perfect. There is no requirement that says you must learn violin or guitar or any other instrument that requires many years of instruction to play. There is one instrument that even the non-musician can pick up and play and that we all have access to, though: the drum. If you really want to master it, you must spend time learning the intricacies of it. There are many kinds of drums and many cultures that use them. Different drums require different playing techniques. There are master players in each culture, and they amaze and inspire with their subtle techniques. But the most basic heartbeat rhythm is accessible to everyone. For the purposes of developing and deepening your spiritual path, the heartbeat rhythm is all that is necessary. A heartbeat rhythm connects us to the source of our physical existence in this body. Our heartbeat is a key to the door to our inner being, and playing a heartbeat rhythm on the drum is a powerful, symbolic way of connecting to the sacred wisdom within.

The drum has gained extreme popularity in the West over the past 30 years. It has been used to provide access to the Spirit World for thousands of years. Indigenous cultures around the world recognize the use of the drum as a powerful spiritual tool that can be used to awaken and heal our spiritual, mental and physical bodies. These types of practices were an intricate part of life in past millennia and now have become largely forgotten. As a result, many in our culture are at a loss as to how to access our natural connection with our inner self.

Specifically, the drum provides us a path of becoming. You can use the drum as a tool for your own awakening.

It is a simple path, but never underestimate the power of simplicity—how such a simple instrument made from nature can be a very powerful instrument of transformation in the lives of humans. Playing the drum in a sacred context can empower you to rediscover the Master Within.

Music and the Imagination

A path of becoming should be conceived as a practice of using the imagination to produce transformative actions. Imagination is the shaping of consciousness into specific sets of images at will. We have long been taught that our imagination is a product of our mind. It is closely associated with creativity and has been placed in a system that allocates them both to left-brain activities. This system is based in science, but science falls short of an adequate and productive definition. Our imagination resides in our heart. We use the mind to develop the thought of having the intention to engage our imagination. After that we disengage the mind and allow the heart to take us deeper into the dimension of the imagination. It is a place beyond the mind and a place where images provide us access to the spiritual worlds.

Images have been used for thousands of years to help us re-create our reality and manifest transformation. We can use visualization and imagination to create a foundation for abstract theories and ideas to manifest into real-life experiences. Imagination allows our perceptions to expand, embrace unseen dimensions, perceive alternate realities and break from the things we take for granted. It encourages us to make critical judgments and gives us the opportunity to "see" beyond the mainstream constructs of society.

Our spiritual practice should engage the use of the imagination to release us from the mundane and obvious, to allow our spirit to inform our perceptions. Music provides a direct connection to our imagination and allows for new patterns to emerge. When we utilize music and imagery, we create a strong and powerful connection to our imagination. There we manifest in the physical what we create in the invisible. Empowering activities, such as yoga, walking, or any other kind of exercise, done in conjunction with engagement of the imagination to visualize the desired state will be enhanced and supported when music is used.

The Magic of Music

While playing music, we can feel a keen sense of intuition that produces a feeling of existing in multiple realities. We are here in the present, in the material world, and we are accessing invisible worlds within and outside our being. We are accessing realities that utilize the intuitive and offer new perceptions. This combination encourages us to develop these faculties of intuition and perception and allows us to receive spiritual wisdom. Learning music aids in developing a deeper and more meaningful sense of who we are and what we are capable of. The development of these faculties will help us navigate life and enable us to create creative, imaginative and wise ways of perceiving and dealing with the world around us.

Playing music in community creates an intimate connection to others and provides an excellent example of how people become engaged in meaningful participation. In looking at music as a paradigm for social intercourse, we find that through the act of music-making, one experiences a sense of togetherness and a connection with others that is at the center of all possible communication.

Music helps us create realities that resist the consciousness of the mainstream. It allows us to form perceptions that are outside the fixed social framework and provides us the option to view the world from alternate perspectives and encourage imaginative creations, which enable growth and change. People engaging in the music will be less likely to conform to the mainstream ideology. We can form foundations in alternate possibilities for the future that place the value of a spiritual path that includes humans, flora, fauna and the earth ahead of the desire for economic and political power. The development of musical awareness embraces a practice of spiritual skills that enable us to create deep and meaningful experiences on a spiritual path.

Music offers us silence as a teacher and guides us to the present moment, where life is born and the future is transformed. Music is metaphor born into reality, where silence is played out in a theater of intentional sound. When we play music, it is important that we respect the space between the notes. Without this silence, music would be noise and without pause. Silence helps us make sense of the music, and silence can help us make sense of our intentions. It offers us clarity and strengthens our connection to the divine.

Enter the Now and Open to the Magic
of the Universe

The tree that offers us the fruit of our intention
came from the seed
of the present moment.

Being in the present moment reminds us of who we are. We are not what we think. As long as we associate ourselves with the mind, we will be in a state of suffering. Being in the present moment offers us opportunities to experience detachment, and paradoxically it also requires detachment.

Detachment is a deep sense of love and compassion that allows all to be as it is. Detachment provides us the ability to remain flexible and deeply rooted in that which we are. It allows us not to be distracted by anything that could potentially take us away from our path and to be deeply involved in every moment in a sincere and meaningful way. Detachment provides us the opportunity to co-create our reality, to manifest our lives into reality, to exist fully as we naturally are—authentic, pure, whole and complete—and to end unconscious resistance to all that is.

The present moment contains everything you will ever need, want or desire. It is up to you to choose where you are going and how you will get there. It is a paradox: You are already there when you are in the present moment.

Consider the following activities to cultivate a deeper and more meaningful relationship with music and the present moment.

Using passive or active meditations can provide higher states of consciousness and greater mental, emotional and spiritual well-being. Passive meditations are ones in which the physical body does not move—e.g., most Zen and transcendental meditations. Active meditations are ones in which the physical body is active and include drumming meditations, walking meditations and dancing meditations. Utilizing music in your walking and dancing meditations will further strengthen your intention and allow you to go deeper. Meditations are useful in getting us within close proximity to silence and the invisible. The invisible holds the key to the wisdom of the Universe.

Active Meditations:

Practice a drumming meditation regularly. Drumming can be a powerful way to connect to your inner wisdom, and at the very least it can allow you to develop the ability to stay out of the mind for extended periods of time. Set aside some time every day or a couple of times a week to spend with your drum. Begin to think of your drum as a living being. If it is made of natural wood and animal hide, it is a living being. The energy and spirit of the tree and animal live inside your drum. When you play that drum, you are calling on the service of the life of the tree and the animal. They are there for you, to help you find the path to your inner being.

Passive Meditations:

Develop a body-focused passive meditation. Focus all your attention on a specific point on your body (your upper lip, just below your nostrils, is a good one). Explore the sensations as you breathe through your nose. Fine-tune your senses. Listen closely to your surroundings. Attune your hearing to perceive the slightest sound in the present moment.

Observe nature in silence. Become one and melt with the plants, trees, rocks and earth. Use your imagination to experience how it might feel to be a cloud, the wind or calm, still air.

Play music at home. Instead of turning the television on for company or recreation, listen to music. Put in your favorite CD or create a mix on your iPod. Listen to music you enjoy; music that touches your heart, inspires you to sing, dance, paint, write or create a creative flow inside your being. For an even deeper experience, listen to music that was created with handmade instruments from natural materials. These naturally made instruments produce frequencies that more easily resonate with you and your energy centers. Over time, you will notice a difference in the way you respond to music played on handmade instruments made from all-natural materials. Listen to music made this way for 30 days, and then go back and listen to music made with synthetic instruments and see if you can tell a difference in the way your physical, mental, emotional and spiritual bodies respond to the music. You may find that when listening to naturally made music, your body responds more quickly to the positive effects of the sound and on deeper levels; you are more easily able to relax and let go of tension.

Sing or chant aloud. When was the last time you sang out loud? There are many opportunities to sing out loud every day. Pick a time that you naturally feel less inhibited, or even better, decide that you don't care who hears you. Sing like no one can hear you, or sing like everyone can hear you, whichever works best for you. Regardless, the most powerful and potent times to sing or chant are when you are in a purposeful, sacred space, such as while meditating with voice or playing music and singing a song. Use your natural voice. Be brave to explore your voice. There is no bad or wrong in your voice and no judgment to be judged by.

One of the first things I realized when I began to listen to indigenous music is that the singers use their natural voices. It was so strange to hear everyday people singing, free of judgments about the quality of their voices. This experience helped me expand my notion of quality to include the energy behind the words. Someone can have a beautiful voice but lack sincerity, and that is not as beautiful as someone with a mediocre voice (by our cultural standards) who sings with deep sincerity and conviction.

Learn a musical instrument. Explore. There are so many kinds of musical instruments in the world, and most can be found on the Web. You can buy an Adungu, a djembe drum, a dunun or a kalimba. You can even find an erhu, a Chinese violin, a soku, a Malian violin, or an ndingidi, a Ugandan violin. See the product page at the end of this book to order instruments.

Observe the Subtleties

The biggest challenge we face in integrating our spiritual path confronts us every day. It seems almost impossible to develop these spiritual practices and virtues within a culture that denies them and bombards us with messages to continually look outside ourselves for answers. Ironically, we see this happening in spiritual circles as well. So many people are searching outside themselves for spiritual enlightenment. So many are traveling to exotic places in search of what is already inside them. It is common for people to travel to participate in the sacred ceremonies of the shaman. Some include the consumption of sacred plants that produce altered states of consciousness. For many, this is the ultimate spiritual experience, and for others it is another stone along the path of the spirit. There may be realizations that come about during one of these sacred ceremonies, and the participant may feel that it was worthwhile and productive. I cannot dispute the experience of anyone, nor am I here to make judgments about the participants or the facilitators of such excursions. That being said, I will say that there are ways to achieve these states and to have these realizations without having to travel, pay fees and ingest psycho-tropic plants.

The answers are right under our noses. They have always been there; they are waiting for us to engage. Without thinking too much about it, we are too quick to think we need to make this big trip to exotic locations, place ourselves around those who call themselves shamans and ingest substances that produce altered states. We are too quick to overlook what we already have inside us. We have been trained to look outside ourselves for everything. We have been trained to think make our determinations of what is possible and what is not possible based on a set of rules that our culture has embraced. Without refection and without question, we disable ourselves into a reality that tells us we may never reach our full spiritual potential and that the path to enlightenment lies outside ourselves in a shaman somewhere or in a plant, book, movie, workshop, class or conversation.

Everything we need is already inside us. Everything we experience contains a message for us. We need to begin listening. It is a process of remembering. Our spirits will awaken as we walk a spiritual path. Navigating the path becomes more fluid when we access the wisdom we have found inside. We are the divinity that we seek, we are the connection that we desire and we are the ones we have been waiting for. Now is the time. Keep walking, keep smiling and enjoy the path. What else is there to do?

CHAPTER TWELVE

The Seven Virtues

These seven virtues are concepts that I believe are vital in developing a spiritual path. Learning how to implement these virtues in our daily lives will require the virtues themselves. Be patient and walk with a passion for a deeper meaning and purpose in your life and you will become everything you wish to be and succeed at all you set out to do.

Humility

I am nobody. I am connected to all beings. My desire to receive is gone. My desire to serve is pure. I am committed to humility. Humility is a deep knowing of who you are, so deep that you have no need or intention to prove anything to anyone, you have no desire to receive recognition. You have lost the ambition you had that fuels your desires and replaced it with a deep sense of humility and a desire to serve. You no longer need anything external to feel happy and content every day.

Humility . . .

• Is letting go of the desire to defend ourselves. When we no longer have anything to protect, we can be in and participate in a state of humility.

Humility . . .

• Be a garbologist; be willing to receive others'

emotional "garbage," transform it into love and give it back as a gift.

Humility . . .

- Is being willing to become "nobody" This culture has taught us very specific definitions of independence, success, and ambition. Redefining these concepts can be a part developing a new belief system that provides a foundation for our spiritual goals.

Humility . . .

- Is always a process and is never complete We ought not to allow ourselves to think we are humble; rather, we should strive to be humble in every moment. Humility is not possessed but requires our participation.

Humility . . .

- Is being willing to have selfless motivation to be the best servant we can be Often, people wish to be a good servant to others but cringe when they are treated like a servant. Sometimes people are humble about receiving something from the exchange. The motivation of a good servant comes from pure humility and therefore should embody a willingness to be treated like one, with nothing to protect and only compassion, forgiveness, gratitude and love to give.

Humility . . .

- Is being willing to listen more and talk less Listening is an effective way to be of service to others. So many times, we are thinking of what we are going to say next while the other person is speaking. Many times we will actually interrupt and say what we think, regardless of whether it was asked for or not. Listening is a practice of humility, and talking less provides us the opportunity to listen deeply.

Whoever has a genuine kind heart
full of humility has kindness
for everyone in every situation.
His or her heart is not darkened
by rudeness, negativity or injustice.

Reflection Questions:

1. What are the consequences of pride?
2. How do we cultivate humility without being taken advantage of?

Steps to Cultivating Humility

- Create a morning mantra for giving thanks for another day on earth. "Thank you, Great Spirit, for another day to be a humble servant, to surrender and die."
- Listen more and talk less.
- Smile for as long as you can.
- Be grateful for all the trials and hard times you have and will experience.
- Practice compassion and forgiveness daily.
- Remind yourself that life is a gift and can be taken at any moment. We are a candle in the wind.

▣   ▣   ▣

Gratitude

How can we create a deep sense of gratitude within our being, one so deep that it forms the foundation of our thoughts and actions? Gratitude resides in unconditional love. The greatest gifts will come when you can begin to cultivate gratitude in every moment.

Gratitude . . .

- Is an acceptance of things just the way they are. Nothing ever goes "wrong," nothing "bad" ever happens. It is our perception that determines our judgments. Gratitude is a position of perception.

Gratitude . . .

- Is the key to a life filled with joy, happiness and contentment. Happiness cannot be looked for, traveled to, possessed, worn or consumed. It is the spiritual experience of living every moment with a deep sense of gratitude.

Gratitude . . .

- Is the end of desire. Being in a state of desire is suffering. Lose desire through gratitude and you will be with the light, always.

Gratitude . . .

- Is alchemy

> *"Gratitude unlocks the fullness of life. It turns what we have into enough, and more. It turns denial into acceptance, chaos into order, and confusion into clarity. ... It turns problems into gifts, failures into success, the unexpected into perfect timing, and mistakes into important events. Gratitude makes sense of our past, brings peace for today and creates a vision for tomorrow."*
> - Melody Beattie

Gratitude . . .

- Is the mother of all other virtues. Participating in gratitude provides us the opportunity to experience a deep sense of compassion, forgiveness, humility, happiness, peace and serenity

"There are no ordinary moments", says Dan Millman, author of The Peaceful Warrior. Dan described a time when his mentor, Socrates, challenged Dan to sit outside on a large flat stone until he had "something of value" to share. Dan sat out on the rock for hours and hours. On more than one occasion, believing he had come up with something, he went to tell Socrates. Each of these times, Socrates decided the statement was not good enough, and he sent Dan back to the rock for more hours of pondering. Finally, Dan had an insight that he knew was something of value. When Dan shared this insight, Socrates looked up, smiled, and welcomed Dan back inside. The "something of value" that Dan had realized was this: "There are no ordinary moments." This is the essence of gratitude. No moment, nothing in life, should be taken for granted. In developing gratitude for every moment—for the simple joys, and even for the challenging times in our lives—we come to truly enjoy and appreciate life. Then we are able to see the magic that surrounds us every second of every minute of every day.

We can have gratitude so deep within that it forms the foundation of our thoughts and actions.

Here are a few things you can do to cultivate a deep send of gratitude.

1. Create a morning mantra to give thanks for another day on earth.

"Thank you, Great Spirit, for another day to be a humble servant to all beings and Mother Earth."

2. Be mindful of taking moments throughout the day to remind yourself to be grateful.

3. Challenge yourself to be grateful for the things that do not appear to be positive in your life, all the things that went "wrong" today or all the "bad' things that happened.

If you notice negative emotions arise in you, stop, breathe and be grateful that you are feeling them. They are messengers, and gratitude is the key to receiving the message.

4. Keep a "gratitude journal." Write all that you are grateful for nightly. Be sure to read past entries each week.

Compassion

How can we have compassion for all beings, especially those we believe have wronged us? How can we experience the mental, emotional and spiritual freedom of practicing compassion every day?

Compassion . . .
- Is allowing ones heart to empathize with another's' experience

Compassion . . .
- Is setting aside one's own ideas of what should be or how another should be and allowing the other to be what he is.

Compassion . . .
Is supporting and refraining from judgment of another's highest good without trying to dictate our own preferences.

Compassion . . .

- Is understanding others' pain, appreciating their joys, wishing the best for them. It does not mean one becomes a "pushover," but compassion does free us to give without fear, because compassion is unconditional; it is not based on reciprocal actions.

When is helping others a disservice?

Compassion can express itself by withholding as well. Sometimes we have to remove physical support if that actually helps our beloved learn something for his highest good. Through compassion, one seeks wisdom in responding—"What really serves this situation?" The answer is not always in doing what a beloved asks; sometimes it is in what serves his spirit. The answer is not always obvious. If one's heart is clear, caring and open, though, the intention at least will have a healing effect.

How can we remain caring, loving and detached?
In cultivating compassion, one has to let go of attachments, because it is difficult to see another's world if our perception is distorted by our own wishes. We have to distance ourselves from our own fear and desire in or-

der to be free enough to see someone else's perspective. In the active practice of compassion, it is also often that we have to let go of our own comforts, be they psychological or physical.

It feels good to experience compassion. It is a natural state of our hearts. It can really hurt to experience someone else's pain, but that also deepens the heart and reveals a deeper sense of connection to our brothers, our planet, and our universe. One broadens, so though there can be pain, the sense of love and connectedness far enriches one's heart and one usually cannot help but want to give more.

Forgiveness

There must be a desire for it and then a decision. Intention must intersect desire to cultivate a deep sense of love and gratitude toward self and others. Forgiveness resides in Unconditional and Unlimited Love. There must be a sincere desire and pure intention to cultivate a deep sense of love, compassion, humility and gratitude

Three Levels of Forgiveness

- Level I: Decisional Forgiveness, in which we make a conscious decision to forgive.

- Level II: Emotional Forgiveness, in which negative emotions, such as resentment, bitterness, hostility, hatred, anger and fear, are replaced with love, compassion, gratitude and humility. Emotional forgiveness provides us with the opportunity to release negative emotions.

- Level III: Spiritual Forgiveness, in which we choose to become a servant to those we wish to forgive.

To Forgive and Forget

Do we really ever forget? If not, forgiveness has not occurred. It is not a process of cognitively forgetting what took place but rather a willingness to completely let go of the feelings and emotions we experienced. That is not to say we allow ourselves to experience the same situation over and over; rather, we gain wisdom that provides us the tools to create a more positive experience in the future. An unwillingness to forgive implies that we are separate from each other.

Detachment

Detachment . . .
- Is a deep sense of love and compassion that allows all to be as it is.

Detachment . . .
- Provides us the ability to remain flexible yet deeply rooted in who we are.

Detachment . . .
- Allows us not to be distracted by anything that could potentially take us away from our path.

Detachment . . .

- Embodies compassion, forgiveness and unconditional love and allows us to experience a deep sense
  of gratitude and fulfillment regardless of what is
  happening around us.

Detachment . . .

- Allows us to expand our awareness beyond our
  senses.

Detachment . . .

- Allows us to view our actions and reactions from
  the place of an observer, slightly apart from the
  outcome.

Detachment requires us to let go of desires that serve
only us. It is the willingness to release any thoughts
or emotions that distract us from a clear, peaceful and
loving place. When we are able to recognize this inner
peace as more valuable than any worldly outcome, we
experience detachment. It is in this place that lasting joy
and awareness originate.

Helpful Tools:

Visualize yourself as a being of light or air or any quality that is uplifting to help you see that any situation is temporal and not essential to your higher sense of well-being.

Use other tools suitable to your nature to arrive at a peaceful state when it is challenged, such as deep breathing, visualizing a peaceful scenario, reliving a happy memory, dancing, yoga, drumming, and singing. There are as many choices as there are personalities.

Serenity

As one becomes more accustomed to this peaceful poise, the value of it becomes more apparent. From this place comes love, creativity, serenity, and joy. One naturally wishes to cultivate it more. You may find yourself in a traffic jam or facing a stubborn clerk or even an angry associate, and instead of being upset, you may observe yourself instead thinking about the way that flower held the morning light when you were walking. This is not denial or disassociation; it is simply retraining your mind to stay focused on peace. This actually induces a state of awareness that can heighten one's ability to resolve conflict. A clear, happy and serene mind allows you to make more informed decisions; your system will function better in the absence of stress.

Oftentimes when I teach a class or give a presentation, I tell the audience members that they have the right to be happy and content for the next two hours or however long the class or presentation runs. I advise them that if anything comes into their heads that says otherwise, it is their right to ask it to leave and they have the option to tell it to come back at a later time. The point of this is to remind people that they are in charge of the show or the gig that is their life. Our emotions and our minds can be useful tools, or they can be the master and the ringleader of the circus mind show. The show that never stops delivering extreme highs and extreme lows.

You have a right to be happy and feel long-lasting joy, serenity and inner peace. Who taught you that happiness and inner peace is something for other people, somewhere else? Being happy and content and feeling joy is a choice. You need to be proactive in creating joy in your life. This is not something that just happens to people. We are not at the mercy of life events that create either pleasurable or un-pleasurable experiences. Our contentment and inner peace do not rely on external stimuli.

Happiness, contentment and inner peace are a choice we should make every day. Really, there is nothing to do but experience them. We do not need to fight for anything, struggle for anything; all we need to do is surrender to being happy. This is the ultimate paradox of the spiritual path. The realization that the key to inner peace is in doing nothing and just being who you are. It is a deep sense of surrender to all that is as it is with the wisdom of compassion and unconditional love. Serenity is a product of detachment. There is no peace in opposition. This requires us to release the desire to defend our position or perspective. It requires us to let go of the desire to be understood or validated. It requires that we stop entertaining the notion that others must change their actions or thinking.

Happiness, serenity and inner peace are the fifth level of detachment. Experiencing happiness, peace and serenity means you have put into action all the lessons you have learned about gratitude, forgiveness, humility and love. These virtues have become your tools to unlock the door to Happiness, Peace and Serenity.

Here are some questions for you to answer and reflect about happiness.

- What is happiness for you?
- What is the origin of happiness?
- Do you experience happiness through emotions or physical sensations?
- What would have to happen for you to be happy in every moment?
- What are the benefits of being happy in every moment?
- How and when will you decide to be happy?
- What would you miss about losing anger, sadness, resentment, shame, etc.?
- What is peace for you?

- What is serenity for you?
- Are you ready for inner peace and contentment?
- How will you cultivate happiness, peace and serenity in your life?
- How will others react to your decision to be happy?

Unconditional Love

Unconditional love is the kind of love a hummingbird has for its young. It is the energy that all living beings are created with. It is the energy that gives you breath. Unconditional love is the most powerful force in the universe. It does not know limitations of any kind. It is unlimited, boundless and eternal. When a being embodies all other six virtues, he will also embody unconditional love. Until then, we can practice unconditional love by also practicing the other six virtues moment by moment.

Martin Klabunde is a professional musician, author and a Nahual initiated in the Zapotec tradition. His mission is to provide a path of awakening through music. With over 20 years of teaching, performance, and workshop facilitation experience, Martin has helped people from all walks of life to achieve inner peace and heightened awareness through an intentional use of music.

In addition to his extensive exposure to the healing ceremonies and traditional rites of passage in East and West Africa, Martin has been taught the ancient rites of Portal Drumming.

In 2009, Martin founded Collective Awakening, an organization committed to providing pathways for spiritual awakening to all people. Integrating his unique experience in music and healing, along with his own spiritual awakening, Martin brings a wealth of artistry, knowledge and wisdom to his music, writing and the workshops and retreats he facilitates around the country.

Additional Books and Essays
by Martin Klabunde

- Learn to Play the Adungu! (2011)
- Reclaiming an Indigenous Voice in Uganda (2004)
- What's the Problem with Development? (2003)
- A Journey to West Africa (1999)
- West African Rhythm Sourcebook (1999)

To order books, music or instruments
visit www.collectiveawakening.us
or email now@collectiveawakening.us

Reaching Higher States of Consciousness™
Through an Intentional Use of Music.

Music available in CD and mp3 format

Adungu Music for Yoga and Massage - Martin Klabunde. Soothing harps, tibetan bowls and soft drums for a relaxing atmosphere.

The Shaman's Drum - Martin Klabunde Native American style drumming, with didgeridoo and percussion create a multi-layered atmosphere for this guided meditation.

From the Heart - Martin Klabunde Original songs featuring the beautiful sounds of the bass and melodic Adungus blended with percussion and vocals.

Loving Kindness Meditation - Martin Klabunde and Wing Man Rita Law A guided meditation for developing Loving Kindness for all beings. Wing Man leads the meditation.

Portal Opening - Martin Klabunde Original rhythms using traditional African instruments. All tracks are percussion based.

Kalumba - Martin Klabunde and Kinobe A beautiful combination of original vocals, East African strings and kalimbas and West African percussion.

The Instruments used on our CD's.
Each is hand made by master craftsmen.

The Adungu is an arched bow harp made of wood and cowhide. It is traditionally played by the Acholi and the Alur people of Northern Uganda.

The Akogo is a kalimba or thumb piano made of wood and metal tines. It is traditionally played by the Teso people of Eastern Uganda.

The Djembe is a drum from West Africa made of native hard woods and goat skin. It is traditionally played by the Malinke and the Bamana people of modern day Guinea and Mali.

Dunun is the name for a family of West African bass drums that developed alongside the djembe in the Mande drum ensemble.

The Didgeridoo is a wind instrument developed by Indigenous Australians of northern Australia at least 1,500 years ago and is still in widespread usage today both in Australia and around the world.

The Pow Wow Drum is a Native American drum traditionally played at a Pow Wow festival and ceremony. This sacred drum is played by multiple people while singing and chanting songs to honor the sacred in life.

The Tibetan Bowls were traditionally used throughout Asia as part of Bön and Tantric Buddhist sadhana. Today they are employed worldwide both within and without these spiritual traditions, for meditation, trance induction, relaxation, healthcare, personal well-being and religious practice.

The Native American Flute was originally very personal; its music was played without accompaniment in courtship, healing, meditation, and spiritual rituals. Now it is played solo, in many different styles of music.

Made in the USA
San Bernardino, CA
06 December 2019